Welcome Home

*For Fran
from Elizabeth*

Tips for
Creating a Haven
for Mind, Body, and Spirit

Elizabeth Knight

**STOREY
BOOKS**

Schoolhouse Road
Pownal, Vermont 05261

The mission of Storey Communications is to serve our customers by publishing practical information that encourages personal independence in harmony with the environment.

Edited by Deborah Balmuth and Robin Catalano
Cover design by Meredith Maker
Cover and interior illustrations by Carleen Powell
Text design by Susan Bernier
Text production by Jennifer Jepson Smith
Indexed by Susan Olason, Indexes & Knowledge Maps

The information in this book is true and complete to the best of our knowledge. All recommendations are made without guarantee on the part of the author or Storey Books. The author and publisher disclaim any liability in connection with the use of this information. For additional information please contact Storey Books, Schoolhouse Road, Pownal, Vermont 05261.

Storey books are available for special premium and promotional uses and for customized editions. For further information, please call Storey's Custom Publishing Department at 1-800-793-9396.

Printed in the United States by R.R. Donnelley
10 9 8 7 6 5 4 3 2 1

Library of Congress Cataloging-in-Publication Data

Knight, Elizabeth D., 1948–
   Welcome Home : tips for creating a haven for mind, body, and
      spirit / Elizabeth Knight.
     p. cm.
   Includes index.
   ISBN 1-58017-187-7 (alk. paper)
   1. Interior decoration—Human factors.   2. Interior decoration—
Psychological aspects.   I. Title.
   NK2113.K575   2000
   747—dc21   99-041601
                                                CIP

Contents

Preface ᴖ iv

Introduction: There's No Place Like Home ᴖ 1

Chapter 1
"Plenty and Grace Be to This Place":
Housewarmings ᴖ 5

Chapter 2
Comings and Goings:
Entrances and Exits ᴖ 24

Chapter 3
Gathering Places: The Living Room,
Dining Room, and Kitchen ᴖ 41

Chapter 4
Private Lives: Bedrooms
and Bathrooms ᴖ 64

Chapter 5
Home Run: Creating a Work Environment ᴖ 88

Chapter 6
Home Away from Home:
Temporary Quarters ᴖ 99

Chapter 7
Inside Out: Window Boxes,
Balconies, Decks, and Gardens ᴖ 118

Chapter 8
Moving Out and Moving On ᴖ 137

Index ᴖ 153

Preface

*Where we love is home. Home that
our feet may leave but not our hearts.*

— Oliver Wendell Homes, Jr.

When I was growing up my father was a career Air Force officer and, like so many military families, we found ourselves on the move quite often. We were transferred, on average, every three years. One memorable year our mail was delivered to El Paso, Texas; Dover, Delaware; and Taranto, Italy!

As an adult, I moved from the family townhouse in Ohio to my first apartment in Florida, on to a fifth floor walkup in New York, and finally to urban New Jersey. I thought my moving days were over, but three months after my husband and I bought a down-at-the-heel country house, he accepted a temporary job assignment in London, and off we went. Now, back on this side of the Atlantic, we divide our time between our Hoboken apartment and our house on Basket Brook.

For some, anyplace they hang their hat is home. For me, home is where the heart lives. This book will share the tips and traditions I've gathered in my topsy-turvy life for making any place, even a furnished flat, feel like home. I hope it will inspire and encourage you to make yourself at home wherever you are.

There's No Place Like Home

A comfortable house is a great source of happiness. It ranks immediately after health and a good conscience.

— Sydney Smith

D o you remember the scene in *The Wizard of Oz* when Dorothy discovers that she can whisk herself back to Kansas merely by clicking together the heels of her ruby slippers and whispering, "There's no place like home?" The power of that simple spell shows us how much we cherish the notion of home. A house is made of bricks and mortar, but a home is a special dwelling where love lives.

Most Europeans and North Americans use the word "house" to describe a dwelling when what they really mean is home. But homes are not always houses. Home to an Inuit on a hunting trip might be an igloo, a temporary shelter cleverly constructed of frozen snow. Home could be a portable lodging such as a desert-dwelling Bedouin's wool tent or a Mongol herder's round felt yurt. Some Plains Indians lived in communal thatched huts, but used a collapsible buffalo-hide tepee on hunting expeditions.

Viking raiders, seafaring explorers, sailors, and whalers successfully lived and worked on ships for long periods of time. Houseboats have been permanent homes to generations of transient people. Chinese pilots ply rivers and canals, as did their ancestors, in wooden workboats, called junks, which house their families and trade goods. Conestoga wagons were mobile homes for homesteaders on their way west.

Some homes are fixed and fortified. A fortress is a house protected by a stone or timber enclosure. A castle is an elite fortress, sometimes isolated by a moat, designed to impress visitors with the owner's wealth, power, and social status. A palace is a pretentious home that took its name from Rome's Palatine Hill where Emperor Nero commanded the building of a splendid home for himself.

Long before the log cabin was lodging for lumberjacks, it was a practical home for medieval Russians and Swedes. Woodsmen hacked out snug dwellings from vast forests by stacking logs one upon another and sealing chinks with mud, moss, or plaster. The New England saltbox house is another form of American domestic architecture with roots in European peasant dwellings.

What is Home?

Now that we have entered a new millennium what is our notion of home? People still need a safe haven that shelters and protects, but physical warmth is no longer enough. We expect the place we call home to warm the cockles of our hearts and provide an intimate and emotionally satisfying setting for our inner and outer life. Home should be a snug, soothing refuge where we can escape the stress of our busy lives and welcome family and friends. Whether it's a house or an apartment, cottage or castle, we all want our homes to be a comfortable place to put up our feet and lay down our heads.

Make Yourself at Home!

Trendspotters observe that many high-flying workaholics who spend a great deal of time away from home create houses with a host of hedonistic comforts similar to those found in luxury hotels, such as voice-sensitive lighting, plush carpets, and even massage rooms. Other people don't want to wait all year for a brief two weeks off to live it up; they'd like to feel as though they're on vacation when they arrive home after a hard day. Because of this shift in attitude, forecasters predict that we'll see an increase in residences with amenities such as pools, jacuzzis, his-and-hers bathrooms, and personal gyms that will make us feel pampered 365 days a year.

In addition to being a wonderful, nuturing haven, we want our home to express something of our taste, interests, and personality. We know that an aesthetically satisfying home is one that engages multiple senses. Sight tends to dominate, but we're increasingly sensitive to the pleasures of furnishing with engaging textures such as a rough sisal rug or a smooth leather sofa. We savor soothing sounds — tinkling wind chimes, gurgling fountains, and the steady tick-tock of a grandfather clock.

Synthetic cleansers and polishes are giving way to the sweet natural fragrances and cleaning power of lavender, citrus, and beeswax that are nicer to our noses and the environment. As we step into the future we're not afraid to refer to our past and draw on ancient wisdom, like *feng shui,* the three-thousand-year-old Chinese art of "auspicious placement."

As we aspire to create a home that marries beauty, practicality, personal expression, and creature comforts, the old rigid rules have been replaced with the attitude that anything goes — as long as it looks good, suits our individual needs, and makes us feel at home. As Louis L'Amour once said, "To build a house is one thing, but to make it a home is quite another."

❧ 1 ❧

"Plenty and Grace Be to This Place"
Housewarmings

Home's not merely four square walls,
tho with pictures hung and guilded;
Home is where affection calls, filled with
shrines the heart hath builded.

— Charles Swain

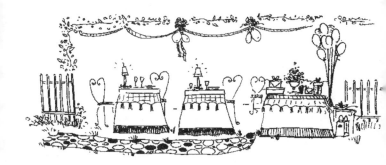

From the beginning of time, in caves and castles, people have marked the special days of their lives — birth, death, coming-of-age, and marriage. There are ceremonies to honor ancestors and rituals to give thanks to the gods for successful hunts or an abundant harvest. Celebrations were created because there is an age-old human need to attach meaning to life and share our experiences with others.

One of humanity's oldest celebrations is a housewarming. Before the Chrisitan era, homes were ritually purified as people gathered to seek protection from evil spirits and give thanks for safe shelter. Later, homes were blessed and dedicated to God. Today, a housewarming is a joyful, symbolic action to acknowledge that you've left behind one home and begun another.

Holding a Housewarming

If you're feeling "rudely moved," a special ceremony, public or private, will ease the transition and help you settle in. If you've had an easy move and are already feeling at home, celebrate your good fortune! Many folks throw a party inviting old and new neighbors, family, and friends to wish them well. Some sanctify their homes with a religious blessing. Others fling open all the doors and windows to air the place out physically and symbolically. Secular or religious, formal or casual, serious or silly, it doesn't matter what you do or how you do it, as long as you do *something* to make your new home feel like it's yours.

Festive First Fire

The hearth, source of light and warmth, has always been a sacred space. In ancient times, when the eldest son married, our ancestors gave him a firebrand from the family hearth to kindle a fire in his new home. Coals from a city's public hearth were carried by citizens founding a new city.

You might hold a real housewarming by lighting a ceremonial first fire in your fireplace or barbecue grill. If you've saved a small log from your old fireplace, use it to start the new fire or ask friends and neighbors to contribute a piece of wood.

According to European folklore, burn pine logs to attract money; add juniper, sage, or tansy for protection against evil spirits.

Sometimes pagan Greeks and Romans wrote prayers on scraps of paper and tossed them on the fire in hopes that the smoke would deliver their messages directly to the deities. You could draw on this tradition by cutting simple house shapes from construction paper. Invite family and friends to write their hopes or wishes on the paper house. Toss the cutouts on the fire and imagine the wishes wafting straight to the higher powers.

> *The holiest sanctuary is the home.*
> *The family altar is more venerable*
> *than that of a cathedral.*
> *The education of the soul for*
> *eternity should begin and be*
> *carried on at the fireside.*
>
> — Richard Baxter

If you haven't got a fireplace, fire up the oven! The Chinese kitchen god, Tsao-wang, guards the hearth and reports the family's behavior to the Jade Emperor once a year on the twenty-third night of the twelfth moon. On his feast day, the family gathers in the kitchen to offer cakes and other goodies to his image so that he'll make a sweet report. You might ritually sweeten your new kitchen by cooking pancakes on a freshly scrubbed griddle. Serve them up with plenty of honey or maple syrup.

As a further taste of good things to come, make a special dinner including rice and beans, symbols of prosperity in many traditions. Add some leafy greenbacks in the form of spinach or lettuce to glean good luck and riches. Asian families strive for a bountiful balance of flavors — sweet and savory — representing pleasure and pain, just like real life. Drink a toast to peace and happiness, clinking glasses together to produce a church-bell-like ring said to terrorize the devil.

Create Your Own Traditions

If you haven't grown up with a housewarming tradition or find that the family ritual doesn't fit your circumstances, feel free to create a new way to celebrate. Examine the myths, superstitions, and customs of other cultures for inspiration. Ask neighbors and friends to share their moving stories. Mix and match to make a meaningful ceremony.

Some form of light, a salute to the sun, the source of all life, has always marked festive occasions. Create a circle of votive candles in glass holders on your living-room floor or outdoors on the ground. Ask each guest to light one and wish you well out loud or in his or her heart.

Visualization is a powerful tool. Sit down with a pile of magazines and rip out pictures and words describing events or feelings you hope to experience in your new home. Whatever your fancy, cut out appealing images and words like "fun," "peace," "joy," "contentment," "comfort," "success," and "prosperity." Assemble a collage, then frame it nicely and hang it up where you can see it first thing every morning.

In the Middle Ages there were few maps of England, so once a year, on Rogation Sunday, villagers walked around the parish grounds "beating the bounds" with willow wands to mark the extent of their territory and commit it to memory. Take a drive around your new territory and mark the boundaries on an official map. Help kids find their feet by walking around the neighborhood and drawing a map complete with landmarks such as a park or video store.

If you have a yard, stake your claim by pounding in pegs at boundary points and festooning them with bright red ribbons. The color of blood is a powerful symbol of energy, strength, and prosperity.

In Scotland, the first person to cross the threshold at midnight on New Year's Eve is said to predict the household's fortune for the coming year. Take a tip from the Scots and invite neighbors, family, and friends to "first-foot" you at an open house party. Ask everyone who crosses your threshold to make an offering of food, drink, or warm wishes. Pay close attention to the actual first footer. A dark-haired man is said to be the luckiest guest; a red-headed woman the least!

Be sure to have a guest book for people to sign; it'll make a great memento of the big day. Alternatively, take a Polaroid of each visitor and have him or her scribble a sentiment on it. After the party, collect the images into an album.

A circle is a universal symbol of unity without beginning or end. Celebrate your relationships! When all your housewarming guests have arrived, gather them into a circle to bind old and new friends. Thank them for helping you feel at home and lead them in a ring dance spiraling in two directions — one for the past, and the opposite for the future.

Long before telephones and e-mail, bells were a major form of communication. It was even said that the reverberations of ringing bells could drive away devils, put out fires, divert thunderstorms, and purify air after an epidemic! In Japan, temple bells toll 108 times at midnight on New Year's Eve to rid the world of the 108 human weaknesses cataloged by Buddha. Invite relatives, friends, and neighbors to a rambunctious housewarming party to ring out the old and ring in the new. When you've achieved critical mass, lead a parade around your place, encouraging everyone to clang bells, bang drums, or toot horns to blast away bad energy.

Host an At-Home Tea Party

If a noisy affair is not your style, opt for a revival of the genteel Victorian "at-home tea." Intimate, practical, and unique, a tea party is the ultimate form of hospitality. Mrs. Isabella Beeton, in her 1888 *The Book of Household Management,* recommended this "useful form of entertainment" for "hostesses with many calls upon their time and a large circle of acquaintances." Sound like you?

Step 1: Set aside an afternoon to receive guests in your new home between three and five o'clock. Call or write to invite folks to join you for "the cup that cheers" and ask them to bring their own cup and saucer. Everyone will have a story to share about why that particular cup was chosen and you'll save on the washing up.

Step 2: Gather food to serve at the event. The menu for this sort of party is usually an elegant snack rather than a meal. Typically it includes three to five kinds of finger sandwiches, scones, assorted pastries (tiny cookies, tarts, or petits fours), and possibly a fruitcake or elaborate, iced, layer cake. If you don't like to cook, everything except the tea can be purchased.

Step 3: Set the scene. For a large group, lay the dining table buffet style with your laciest linens and daintiest china. A smaller number of guests may be seated around the table or served from a sideboard, coffee table, or butler's tray.

For more ideas and details on how to conduct a tea party consult my book *Tea with Friends* (Storey Books, 1998).

Charm Your Guests

Janus, the Roman god with two faces who watched over entrances and exits, held the keys to both the future and the past. We've all heard of ceremonies in which a mayor or other dignitary formally presented a celebrity with the keys to the city. This comes from the custom of a city surrendering its keys to the enemy who had captured it. How about awarding family members and friends, who have captured your heart, a symbolic key to your new home? Simply collect old keys or cut out cardboard ones and thread them on bright red ribbons.

Myths tell of supernatural beasts who ferociously guarded the entrances to palaces and sacred spaces. Look for a protective lion's head or paw, dragon, or dog-shaped door knocker. Ceremoniously mount it on your front door and invite guests to knock three times while making an auspicious wish for your new home. The power of the number three is universal to all times and cultures. Some believe the number represents body, soul, and spirit; to others heaven, earth, and water.

In Islamic cultures, a hand, symbol of protection and strength, is painted or carved onto the door to push away the evil eye. For a simple housewarming ceremony, ask guests to dip a hand in water and press their palms to the front door to bless your new home.

To feather your new nest, hand guests feather-shaped pieces of construction paper and provide pens for them to write wishes. Gather the paper slips in a bowl or nest.

A BRIEF GUIDE TO SYMBOLS

Every culture has symbols that express good or provide protection. Here are some traditional symbols you could incorporate into your housewarming ceremony; keep them in mind when you choose a gift to welcome a new neighbor!

SYMBOL	MEANING
teapot	hospitality
angel	God's guidance
house	protection
bird	joy
rose or heart	love
fruit basket	generosity
fish	plenty
flower basket	good wishes

Because a live chick bursts forth from what appears to be a lifeless stone, the egg is an ancient symbol of hope and rebirth. To celebrate your rebirth in a new place, hollow out the shells of a clutch of eggs. Invite family and friends to carefully draw a symbol of their good wishes on an egg with a marker. Dye the eggshells red and bury them in an auspicious spot such as by a gatepost or door. If you live in an apartment building, place the eggs in a basket near the entrance to strengthen your nesting instincts.

Hang a horseshoe from the eaves or mount one on your front door. Wicked witches and warlocks were said to be afraid of iron, and legends persist that the house to which the shoe is attached will prosper. Make sure the shoe is turned upward; the crescent shape represents the moon goddess, and the two horns secure her power and protection.

Hide a bottle stuffed with nine nails, nine needles, and nine pins in the rafters to spook sprites with mischief on their minds.

Hold a House Blessing

Gwen Steege, a friend, shared a wedding ritual that could be adapted to make a lovely housewarming ceremony. Her son and his bride, who are potters, made a pair of beautiful bowls. The larger one was used to create a fountain; the smaller was filled with water from a nearby river.

Guests scooped water from the little bowl into the larger one while uttering a prayer or special wish. After the wedding, the fountain served as a visual reminder that friends' blessings flow through the couple's home and lives.

Time capsules are trendy again, and they're not just for kids. Fill a bottle, or a polymer tube made for the purpose, with memorabilia to make a gift of the present for future generations. Choose items from the sublime to the ridiculous that have personal significance. Write or type a note rather than include a recorded message which might be unintelligible in future years. Hold a formal sealing ceremony and take photos for your memory book. Remember to record the capsule's location.

Many Eastern European cultures offer gifts of bread, candles, and salt to new households. The bread symbolizes abundance, the candles light and warmth, and the salt enduring wisdom. Arabs maintain that once you have shared salt with your host you are honor bound never to harm him. Japanese sumo wrestlers sprinkle salt on the ground to purify it before beginning a bout. Some people ritually place a pinch of salt in the corner of every room to cleanse a new house.

Not so long ago, people invited their parish priest, minister, or spiritual guide to sanctify new homes with a religious blessing.

It is an ancient Native American practice to make an offering or say a prayer at each point of the compass. You might ceremoniously cleanse your new dwelling by pouring water in each of the four corners of your house or in four directions in the yard and chant the prayer to "the North for greatness, the East for health, the South for neatness, the West for wealth."

Greek Orthodox priests use basil dipped in holy water and olive oil for their house blessings. Jews hold a dedication ceremony, then attach a mezuzah, a decorative holder for a scroll bearing two quotes from Deuteronomy, just outside the front door.

I've roamed through many a
weary round,
I've wandered east and west,
Pleasure in every clime I found,
But sought in vain for rest.
While glory sighs for other spheres,
I feel that one's too wide,
And think the home which
love endears
Worth all the world beside.
The need thus, too rudely moved,
wanders unconscious where,
Till having found the place it loved,
It trembling settles there.

— Thomas Moore

Making a Sacred Space

Every home is a sacred space. Even tent-dwelling nomadic tribes travel with images of gods and ancestors. Romans erected altars to their ancestors and household gods charged with keeping the occupants safe, happy, and healthy. People of many faiths continue this rich tradition today.

Orthodox Greeks have an elaborate *ikonostasi* or household altar, above the bed or in a corner of the living room, displaying religious images, candles, oil, and a bowl of water. Filipinos structure their shrines around images of Santo Niño, the baby Jesus. Buddhists and Hindus offer gifts of food or flowers to the deities represented on their altars. In preparation for their joyful Day of the Dead festival, Mexicans erect colorful altars honoring departed family and friends. A candle represents each soul, but altars are also laden with earthly pleasures such as the deceased's favorite food and drink, toys, tools, books, and clothing.

Create an "Altar"

Even if you're not religious you might like to create a special place in your home to help you focus your thoughts, express emotions, or honor whatever's important to you. Your shrine or altar can be as elaborate a space as resources allow. Some people set aside a whole wall, while some use a shelf or mantel. The location should be permanent even if what's on display changes. Include inspirational poems, personal totems, favorite cartoons, or lucky charms!

If you live far from family, you might like to have what my grandmother called a "rogue's gallery" with photos of absent family and friends wreathed with candles, incense, or flowers. While grieving for a cherished pet, one woman I know gathered her dog's collar, leash, and food bowl next to a photo of the two of them romping on the lawn.

Deep in December, you might display a bowl of beach glass, a lighthouse-shaped candle, and a framed poem about the seashore to tide you over until your next visit.

A friend told me that when her daughter graduated high school, she gave the girl a box containing a pair of severed apron strings. If you have a fledgling leaving the family nest, you and your child could fill a nest or bowl with significant or symbolic objects to be left behind.

TRADITIONAL IRISH BLESSING

God bless this house from roof to floor
God bless the windows and the door
God bless all for evermore
God bless the house with fire and light
God bless each room with thy might
God with thy hand keep us right
God be with us in this dwelling site.

Bring Nature into Your Celebration

To help yourself feel rooted in your new digs, plant a tree. Trees are symbols of regeneration and rebirth; planting a seedling when a baby is born is a ritual that appears in nearly every culture. Thousands of years ago Europeans believed that gods and goddesses inhabited trees. Russian peasants thought that their ancestors lived in birch trees. Today people knock on any piece of wood for luck.

In Greek mythology, oaks were sacred to Thor and Zeus; thus oak seedlings were planted near houses as protection against thunder and lightning. Ash trees were once held in high esteem for their ability to shield the house from snakes. Highlanders traditionally planted a rowan tree beside their houses to repel witches.

Spruce up your garden with an evergreen. Cedar symbolizes healing and longevity. The Japanese say that the pine tree's needlelike leaves drive away demons; this "tree of immortality" also shelters houses and brings joy. Europeans used to plant holly because prickly people settled quarrels beneath the tree. A sprig tied to the bedpost brought happy dreams; a tonic made with the leaves could cure coughs.

> *Bloom where you are planted.*
>
> — Common saying

There are auspicious plants and flowers, too. Scott Cunningham's *The Magical Household* provides these tips: Hydrangeas, sunflowers, and bamboo bestow good luck; mint, onion, snapdragon, camellia, chamomile, clover, dill, basil, and banana plants attract money; hyacinth, lavender, marjoram, catnip, and morning glories make for a happy home. Grow a Norfolk Island pine inside your home and you'll never go to bed hungry. Safeguard your space against thieves with a fence of garlic, cumin, caraway, rosemary, thistles, aspen, cactus, or juniper trees.

Contemporary Housewarmings

Connie Anderson of San Marcos, California, relates that when she and her husband, who was a pastor, moved to one new church, their flock welcomed them with a "pounding." Each parishioner brought a pound of something — sugar, salt, coffee, apples — to help set up their new home. Extend this practice to new neighbors by presenting them with a local newspaper, a box of candy, a flashlight with batteries, or candles and matches.

Ancient Egyptians believed that glittering stars were the homes of spirits. The Blackfoot Indians thought that each star was once a person. Step outside on your first night in your new home and make a wish on the very first star you see. Starry-eyed, take a moment to remember all your ancestors who had the courage to hitch their wagon to a star and start over in a new place.

> *The stars are mansions built by nature's hand, and . . . there the spirits of the blest dwell, clothed in radiance. . . .*
>
> — William Wordsworth

Lani Stack, who's lived in twenty-five places in twenty-three years (her dad was in the Navy) says her family's homemaking tradition revolved around curtains. Even before the boxes were unpacked, her mother would replace the government-issue venetian blinds with homemade curtains. Although wrinkled, they put the family stamp on base housing.

A Guide to Housewarming Gifts

Tradition holds that housewarming gifts should be for the house, not the people who live in it. In addition to a copy of this book, here are some suggestions to help newcomers put down roots:

Decorative garden markers, planter pots, window boxes, seeds, houseplants, and herbs are thougtful gifts for those with a green thumb.

Give an oak seedling with instructions to plant it under a waning moon. The recipient is guaranteed to come into money.

A protective angel, gargoyle, or witch's ball (reflective, old-fashioned garden ornament) are wonderful adornments for a garden or balcony.

A rose bush encourages love to bloom.

Set the stage for a warm welcome with a hibachi or a basket filled with all the fixings for a barbecue.

When a friend moves from an apartment with a high-tech shower to a house with an old-fashioned bathtub, give her crisply starched vintage hand towels and a bar of handcrafted soap as a practical and pretty housewarming gift.

Wind chimes for porch or deck are decorative and pleasing to the ear. Feng shui experts claim sweet-sounding metal chimes attract positive energies.

An oversize hammock is a great way for a new homeowner to take some time out.

One friend told me that her family's tradition is to give a clock as a housewarming gift "to count the happy hours." A sundial could serve the same purpose for a friend with a garden. A personalized house sign would help family and friends claim their new space.

A vase is a symbol of life because it holds the liquid necessary for all life. If you want to fill one with flowers, Eastern European traditionalists would suggest that you include an odd number of blossoms along with your best wishes.

A tool kit with a fix-it book will be appreciated by those who could use a helping hand.

A new broom sweeps clean." A broom is a practical present loaded with lore. If you drop a broom, expect company, but don't step over it or you'll never marry. The traditional besom, made of a bundle of twigs tied to a handle, is said to possess magical power to attract both good fortune and bad luck, depending on how it's handled. Tell the recipient not to lean against a bed or sweep the house at night. Whisking dust out the door or from room to room is also asking for trouble. Happiness will be yours, however, if you remember to sweep to the center of the floor and scoop up dirt with a dustpan.

A wicker picnic basket would be a welcome gift to help the recipient enjoy the great outdoors.

Bird, soft-sigh me home," wrote famous author Theodore Roethke. Swallows, martins, and hummingbirds attract good fortune, so a bird feeder or birdbath is an auspicious gift.

2

Comings and Goings

Entrances and Exits

Shut the door. Not that it lets in the cold but that it lets out the coziness.

— Mark Twain

E veryone knows the importance of a first impression and the satisfaction of a happy ending. Entrances and exits are the first and final impressions we make for our guests and ourselves. A dreary, dimly lit, or cluttered entrance or exit is tricky to traverse and it telegraphs KEEP OUT! You want the first and last impressions to be ones of peace, order, light, and comfort.

Your goal is to make the approach to and departure point from your home easy to find and welcoming. This is the time and the place to hint at the warm haven that waits just beyond the door.

Making an Entrance

We're so accustomed to traipsing in and out that we don't often notice what visitors see. What does the transition from the outside world to your world lead people to expect? Is this visual message a true reflection of your personality and hospitality?

Is the pathway to your door or exit to your yard or driveway an obstacle course? Is the grass trimmed or do you have to wade through a weedy wilderness? Is your walkway or driveway free of potential hazards such as sports equipment, toys, or snaked garden hoses? Are there overgrown shrubs that grab at your guests' clothing as they make their way to the door?

Don't procrastinate when little things need repair. As the saying goes, "He who will not repair a gutter will soon have a house to repair."

Is the informal entrance through a kitchen, laundry room, or garage? If so, make sure the approach is clean, tidy, and navigable even if it's not glamorous. Is there enough room in the garage to get out of the car without skewering yourself on a pair of skis?

Where can company park? Any large cracks or chips in the sidewalk to trip the unsuspecting? If you live in an apartment building, is the hallway leading to your door adequately lit? Are floors and walls clean, without flaking paint or peeling wallpaper? If things aren't up to snuff, write to the landlord or building manager and request an inspection.

The house number on your door should be clear and large enough to be read easily at a distance. Make sure yours is well lit and unobstructed by shrubbery or decorations such as wreaths. If the door is at a distance from the street, post the numbers on a fence or add a curbside sign with your house number.

Mailboxes

Did you zip right by the mailbox without even noticing it? Nowadays we take it for granted, but did you know that free rural mail delivery was not even available before 1896?

A customized mailbox is just part of the first impression you create for your home. Start with the site. Could the mailbox be incorporated into a fence? Or support an outdoor light?

Use Decoration as Self-Expression

Think of the mailbox as a blank canvas and feel free to personalize it with molding, paint, stamps, stencils, and/or found objects to reflect your personality, hobby, or occupation. I know we're getting close to our Catskill Mountains weekend home when I spy the neighbor's mailbox painted black and white in tribute to his dairy cows. If this isn't your style, you could add miniature window boxes and plant with seasonal flowers and foliage.

If the mailbox is mounted on your house, you could paint the surrounding wall and/or box to create a fantasy environment. For example, the Woods family might paint a forest scene featuring a different type of tree for each family member.

Porches and Portals

The porch is a transition zone between public and private space, outdoors and indoors, secular and sacred. The humble porch began life as a *porticus,* a covered walkway on a Greek temple with a roofed entrance girded by columns. The idea was to architecturally mark the passage from the outer profane world into an inner sacred space. Over time, the porticus evolved into a breezy verandah built by colonists in the New World to take advantage of cooling breezes.

Long out of fashion, the porch is once again popular. We've rediscovered the benefits of having an outdoor living room; it's the perfect place to share coffee and conversation with friends or recover from cabin fever in solitary splendor sheltered from sun and rain. Porches can even feature a fireplace to help them span the seasons comfortably or chandeliers for a touch of grandeur.

CROSSING BOUNDARIES

Sometimes the threshold represents a boundary, but it might also be a dangerous border between this world and the next. Myths tell of heroes, such as Hercules and Cuchulainn, who must subdue snarling guard dogs, dragons, lions, or serpents before they may triumphantly stride over a threshold into a world of wonders.

Paleolithic people carved labyrinth designs on cave walls. Later, these designs were painted on houses to confuse evil spirits. During the Middle Ages, garden mazes were constructed for amusement and as a form of physical meditation for the faithful who were unable to go on a pilgrimage; the act of walking the maze was considered to be a form of praying. If gardening is not your strong suit, compensate by painting the porch floor with boat deck paint to simulate a bushy boxwood maze. Part the shrubbery at the center to reveal a beautiful open rose. Or you might create a spiral maze coiled with soothing words such as *calm* or *unwind.*

A rocking chair, hammock, or porch swing is crucial to catching the rhythm of life in the slow lane. Someday, if I ever have a proper porch, I'll paint a tongue-in-cheek cloud scene on its ceiling complete with chubby cherubs scattering rosebuds and trailing a banner that reads WELCOME HOME!

My heritage is both southern and northern; the northern half of me was charmed to discover that there is special porch etiquette in the South. It seems that folks relaxing on a porch are honor bound to extend an invitation to strolling friends to join them, perhaps for a cool drink. But both the porch sitters and the passersby expect the invitation to be refused the first and second time it is issued because it may have been offered merely to be polite. Only when invited for a third time are the passersby truly welcome to mount the porch steps and "sit a spell."

> *The most difficult mountain to cross is the threshold.*
>
> — Danish proverb

Furnishing Your Porch

Furnish your porch with seating that won't be damaged by showers or mildew. Wicker has been a favorite since Victorian times because it is lightweight and easily moved to catch or avoid the sun. Classic finishes are white, dark green, black, or brick-red paint, but you might prefer a rich brown stain. Whatever the finish, keep wicker clean by vacuuming, or dust with a paintbrush sprayed with furniture polish.

Resin, wood, wrought iron, and heavy-gauge wire pieces add interesting textures to the mix. Unify a hodgepodge of mismatched furniture with a coat of enamel paint.

Glass hurricane globes add glamour and protect candle flames from breezes. Unscented candles won't attract insects. Citronella candles shed a soft glow and keep bugs at bay.

A ceiling fan takes up less space than a floor model and there's no cord to trip over.

Nestle a basket of books next to a comfortable armchair. If you have room, add a shelf or book-case. Scour yard and library sales for secondhand classics and light reading. Toss in a book of short stories for short attention spans or a really long novel to work on all summer.

E-mail's handy, but it can't charm with the warmth of a hand-written note. Provide a small basket full of pretty note paper, birthday cards, postcards, pen, and stamps.

Make little ones feel welcome by providing a lid-ded basket or old metal picnic basket packed with books, games, or small toys to amuse them while adults talk.

Install a wall-mounted coat rack next to an umbrella stand for walking sticks, canes, and drippy bumbershoots. A tall, galvanized florist's tin or old, knee-high rubber boot would be interesting alternatives.

Hang wind chimes. In Japan, where summers can be quite humid, the sound of tinkling windchimes is thought to enhance one's appreciation of the barest breeze.

Every porch needs at least one table that can be used as a work surface or for serving snacks. Make a floor-length skirt for a round table from a pretty sheet or piece of canvas. Add a glass tabletop for protection. Stow stackable plastic shoe boxes full of jigsaw puzzles (dot the back of each puzzle with a different color marker or nail polish to prevent pieces from getting mixed up) or hobby or needle-craft projects under the skirt.

An old-fashioned kitchen table with drawers would make a handy porch sideboard. Placemats, cutlery, and napkins could be stashed in a drawer, thus saving trips to the kitchen. Alternatively, use the table to store arts and crafts projects and supplies.

A big wicker hamper could store all-weather furniture covers.

Taking Steps

Capitalize on the natural progression of steps to make a procession to your porch or door. Arrange everything on your stairs from big to little and bottom to top. Add different types of ornamentation, from potted plants to decorative lanterns. Out west, folks line walkways with *farolitos* — small paper bags rolled down a couple of inches, filled with sand, and "planted" with a lit candle — to create a festive feeling. Another idea is to pop tin kitchen graters directly over pillar candles to create patterned pools of light. For safety's sake, you might need to supplement decorative lighting with a stronger porch light.

The Gate or Door

"When one door shuts, another opens," says the old proverb.

A door is a universal symbol of opportunity and transition. Long ago, Romans made sacrifices to Janus, the two-headed gatekeeper god, who held the "keys of power" that he employed to open the door to the New Year. Because this deity could see the future as well as the past, people sought his protection before a journey and gave him thanks for a safe return.

In the Christian faith, St. Peter is said to guard the "pearly gates," swinging them wide to usher the saintly into Heaven. Cathedrals traditionally have three entrances to represent faith, hope, and charity.

Personalizing with Signs and Symbols

In many societies, people safeguard the access to their home by placing amulets or signs on the door. The Incas applied a mixture of grain and human blood to the threshold. The Jewish Passover commemorates a night when Israelites daubed their doors with the blood of a lamb to distinguish their homes from those of the Egyptians, thus protecting God's chosen people from the angel of death. Today, many Jews attach a *mezuzah* (literally, "doorpost"), a decorative holder containing the written tenets of their faith, to doorways or gates.

In the Near East and North Africa a red hand is painted on the portal to push away the evil eye. Similarly, doors and window frames in the American southwest are painted indigo blue to block bad spirits. Greeks and Romans hung horseshoes on house walls to protect themselves from the plague. Many of us still mount a horseshoe over our front door or on a barn beam to catch luck.

Flanking doors with tubs of evergreens is not new. According to Beverly Pagram, author of *Heart & Home,* Mediterraneans traditionally positioned pots of bay leaves on either side of the door for protection from witchcraft and lightning. Greeks believed that those who wrote wishes on the bay leaves could expect them to be granted by Apollo, the god of prophecy.

Rosemary, sacred to the Virgin Mary, is a timeless symbol of friendship and remembrance because of its enduring scent. If you haven't room for pots or tubs you could craft a bay leaf wreath accented with rosemary sprigs to dress up your door.

My door sports a plain brown grapevine wreath that I decorate to reflect the seasons or celebrate an event. My friend Elizabeth Asbury wound a similar wreath with pale blue and ivory satin ribbons and tucked in strawflowers to celebrate the birth of each of her sons.

A flat-backed basket brimming with blossoms is a sunny welcome and doesn't take up much space. It's easy to do: Simply pack the basket with florist's foam cut to fit and anchor dried flower stems in the foam. To maintain fresh flowers for several days, remove the foam and allow it to soak in water, line your basket with a piece of foil or plastic, and repack the foam.

Legend says that those who leave doors ajar will never own a home. So shut that door!

The pineapple is a very old symbol of hospitality. Nineteenth century American sea captains brought the exotic fruit home from the South Seas and mounted them on doors or fence spikes to announce their safe return to the community. You could wire miniature pineapples, clementines, and magnolia leaves to a wreath form. Or, you might prefer a pineapple-shaped door knocker to symbolize your warm welcome.

Anyone can personalize a plain, coconut-fiber doormat. Use a photocopier or computer to create a template of your apartment number or a simple image. Trace the image onto stencil card (from an arts and crafts store) the same size as the mat, and cut it out using a sharp craft knife. Place the stencil on the mat, spray the cutout with enamel spray paint, remove the stencil immediately, and leave to dry thoroughly.

Approach your door as an opportunity to express hospitality and signal something about your heritage. A sweet-sounding bell from my grandfather's shop is attached to the back of our front door. It's a cheerful notice that someone's coming or going. An Irish friend's door wears a plaque inscribed with *Failte,* the traditional Gaelic greeting.

City dwellers might distinguish their apartments' look-alike entryways by painting the door a bright color — glossy apple green, poppy red, or even eggplant purple — as Europeans do. It's a quick, easy, and inexpensive way to impart a little personality. Be sure to check with your landlord before painting, though.

Christen your home with a descriptive or whimsical name such as "Cobweb Cottage," "Hollibell Farm," or "Brook House." In England, the number plaque is often embellished with the name of the house.

> *May the winds of adversity ne'er blow in your door.*
>
> — Scottish toast

A colorful windsock or fluttering flag is said by feng shui experts to express energy and attract friends. You could also hang a bright seasonal banner or playful kite with your name painted on it.

Make an Inviting Hallway

The hall is another transition area, a place to shed the outside world and let the house receive you with a warm welcome. If you don't have a porch, or it's too cold to enjoy it, the entranceway becomes even more important. Think of the hall as a room in its own right rather than merely a pedestrian passageway. Make the first impression count and set the stage by appealing to the senses.

Signal sweet times to come with a fragrant bowl of potpourri, herbs, or flowers. Vervain, mint, and meadowsweet were traditionally used in medieval England as strewing herbs to impart a pleasant fragrance when crushed underfoot and contribute to a healthy and happy atmosphere.

If your hall is narrow and dark, as many are, install extra overhead lighting or boldly paint it a bright color. Yellow is a good color for a corridor that doesn't get much natural light. Or you might paint the hallway a color that links it to the rooms that lead off it, perhaps a lighter shade of the color of an adjoining room.

Hang a shoe bag with plastic pockets on the back of a door to sort mufflers, mittens, and hats in a tight space.

My Aunt Lois painted a large, leafy tree on her hall wall to replace scribbles left by six little ones. Every branch of the family was represented and there was a different bird for each family member. As a teenager, I felt very grown-up when I was allowed to add my own bird to the Knight side of the family tree.

A mirror, or a collection of them, amplifies light, makes a tiny hall look bigger, and is handy for checking your appearance before you greet your visitors.

Keep furniture to a minimum so that the hall is easy to walk through. Aim for a twelve-inch clearance for the door to swing open. A lidded bench, rather than a table, provides a place to drop the dry-cleaning and store sports gear as well as a comfortable spot to sit and remove wet or muddy shoes.

If you have room, add a hutch, cupboard, or chest of drawers. Assign a different drawer or shelf to each household member as a door-side in-out box. Use the top surface for a still life vignette of decorative objects.

A rug or runner adds color and softness as well as an absorbent surface for mud. Secure it with carpet tape or a nonskid pad.

You'll need a "touch-down" surface to catch keys and the mail. If you don't have room for a table, install a shelf deep enough for a small lamp, clock, and a favorite framed photograph or bowl of sweet-smelling potpourri (keep out of reach of children and pets). Visually anchor the shelf with a framed mirror or print above and attractive storage containers below.

If you are lacking a closet, position a coatrack nearby or install coat pegs (kids will need some at their height, too) so you don't have to traipse wet clothing through the living room. To maximize a small space, look for a combination coatrack, shelf, and storage compartment. The coat pegs on these units are mounted on a lid that lifts to reveal space for stowing scarves, hats, and gloves. The deep shelf above the storage compartment can be used as a catchall for keys and mail or as a display area.

Be adaptable. I discovered a six-foot plywood "tree" in a china showroom prop sale for twenty dollars. The addition of twig-shaped pegs turned the prop into a one-of-a-kind coat rack. Positioned in a hall corner this "family tree" hides skis and stacks of canning jars.

Cut down on clean-up by providing a tray for wet footwear next to an umbrella stand.

Making the Most of Stairs

Press every nook and cranny into service. Display a dramatic piece of sculpture or unusual piece of furniture in the dead space under stairs. You could fit a bar or mini-office into this overlooked real estate or use it to hide the controls for a music system.

House bulky sports equipment on hooks or shelves or in drawers beneath the stairs. Close off the area with louvered or plain cupboard doors cut to fit. A less formal solution would be shutters, blinds, curtains, or a folding screen.

Provide a staircase basket for every set of stairs. Designed to fit on any standard step, it will serve as a catchall, saving wasted trips up and down.

Be Creative!

Paintings, prints, and photos aren't all that can be hung on the walls. What do you collect? Decorative masks would brighten a bland entryway. You might display a prized collection of trophy cups or gleaming paperweights on a narrow shelf or window ledge. A changing parade of hats would be a lighthearted way to share your personal passion.

Create a "guard dog" to secure your keys by looping a small, flat-backed pocket basket over a drawer pull or coatrack peg. If you're a dog-lover, take a snapshot of your pooch to a photo shop where the background can be cut away and the resulting image mounted on a plaque. Screw cup hooks into the base.

Place a guest book and pen in a prominent place as is done in bed and breakfast inns. It's comforting to read all the compliments on a day when nothing's gone right. I knew a woman who reserved one office wall for visitor's signatures and graffiti.

3

Gathering Places
The Living Room, Dining Room, and Kitchen

In happy homes he saw the light of household fires gleam warm and bright.

— Henry Wadsworth Longfellow

Homes are divided into private zones and gathering zones. When we emerge from our secluded baths and bedrooms for a big family celebration or plain old Wednesday night dinner, special attention should be given to details. A cozy furniture arrangement around the hearth or a festive table setting sends a loving message to your gathering family and friends.

The Fireplace

A glowing hearth was once the focal point of every home. In fact, *focus* is the Latin word for "hearth." It's hard to imagine, but in the dark days before matches, fire was revered as a gift from the gods. Legend tells of Prometheus, who lit a torch from the chariot of the Sun, thus stealing the immortals' fire to give to humankind.

Ancient Origins

From prehistoric times right up to the late 1880s, the fireplace was the primary means of cooking food and providing light and warmth for the European and American household. Family and friends gathered around the flickering flames for companionship, to tell tales and give advice, and catch up on mending and reading.

Creating a Focal Point

If you're lucky enough to have a wood-burning fireplace, make it the room's focal point. In most stylish eighteenth-century European and American homes, the wall above the fireplace was reserved for an important painting or a large decorative mirror to make the most of natural light.

Today, feng shui experts suggest that you flank the sparkling mirror with plants to encourage the flow of positive energy. Gather deep, cushiony chairs or pillows around the hearth to warm the cockles of your heart on a long winter's night. If you have pets, position a softly lined basket near the fire so they can enjoy a snug snooze.

Always kindle a crackling fire when you are expecting guests as a physical expression of your warm welcome.

Keep a basket of dried citrus peels, which burn a beautiful blue, and aromatic spices such as sandalwood, cinnamon, or cloves to toss into the flames.

Andirons may be old-fashioned, but they enable the burning logs to fall onto a bed of hot coals and burn more efficiently than logs on a raised grate.

WOOD FOR BURNING

Beechwood fires burn bright and clear
If the logs are kept a year;
Chestnut's only good they say
If for years 'tis stored away;
Birch and firwood burn too fast,
Blaze too bright and do not last;
But ashwood green and ashwood brown
Are fit for a queen with a golden crown.

Even a nonfunctioning fireplace can serve as a room's focal point. Hang prints and paintings, punctuated by small sparkling mirrors, on the chimney breast (the exposed area above the mantel) and cluster a disparate collection of candlesticks, unified by the same color candles.

If you don't have a fireplace, create a "hearth" by clustering candles on a shelf, sideboard, or deep windowsill. Magnify their glow by placing them where a mirror or polished metal surface can reflect the flames. Never leave burning candles unattended.

The Kitchen: The House's Warm Heart

The kitchen has always had a magical ability to attract people. Real estate agents claim that houses are often sold on the appearance of the kitchen alone, whether or not the buyer actually intends to spend much time cooking. Realtors even suggest sellers arrange to have the appetizing smells of baking bread and fresh coffee wafting in the air when a prospective buyer is due! And have you ever noticed that at any party, no matter how big the place, everyone eventually gathers in the kitchen?

Involve Your Family and Guests

When I first started to cook for company and was very unsure of my abilities, I wanted everything prepared well in advance and all evidence of my hard work (and charred disasters) cleaned up and put away. It was to look as if the Food Fairy had waved her magic wand, and presto, there was pasta and pesto. Trouble was, by the time the party came around, the Food Fairy needed a nap. Now I know part of the fun is allowing your family and guests to make a contribution so everyone can share in the satisfaction of a wonderful meal.

Even a four-year-old can put napkins and silverware on the table. Kids can practice their social skills by greeting people at the door or hanging up coats. You might ask the first arrivals to help the next wave get settled with a drink. Shy people often like to duck into the kitchen and help prepare a bread basket. Some people don't want to get involved in the food preparation, but they're wonderful at starting the conversational ball rolling. Everybody has something to share — let them!

> *Let your boat of life be light, packed with only what you need — a homely home and simple pleasures, one or two friends, worth the name, someone to love and someone to love you, a cat, a dog, and a pipe or two, enough to eat and enough to wear, and a little more than enough to drink; for thirst is a dangerous thing.*
>
> — Jerome K. Jerome

Using Nature's Bounty

Fresh herbs have much more flavor than dried so if you've got a sunny window start a crop now to flavor soups, stews, salads, and sauces. Every kitchen would also benefit from an aloe plant. European folk wisdom holds that aloe can insulate the household from intruders and accidents. Roman cooks applied aloe to prevent blistering. Squeeze out the leaf's sticky gel to soothe cuts, burns, even insect bites.

Salt has played a fundamental role in history as a food preservative and seasoning. Ancient Greeks, according to Linda Spencer, author of *Knock on Wood,* welcomed guests by placing a pinch of salt on their palms even before offering a glass of wine. Fine-grained, free-flowing salt is best for baking, but many professional chefs prefer the flavor and texture of coarse-grained kosher or sea salt for general cooking.

Ropes of dried garlic, onion, and peppers have been hung in kitchens for several centuries as decoration and as protection against evil spells. Sifters and colanders sieve out bad luck, and mortars and pestles are traditional safeguards as long as you move the pestle in a clockwise, sunwise, motion. Kitchen witches, clad in bright babushkas and sitting astride their brooms, are hung in some modern kitchens as lucky charms.

Fresh, healthy green plants, according to David Daniel Kennedy, author of *Feng Shui Tips for a Better Life* (Storey Books, 1998), bring *chi*, or life energy, into your kitchen and symbolically "feed the fire" of the stove, increasing its strength and brightness. A clean stove with a mirror hung above it generates abundance.

Hot Tips

Place plastic lazy Susans in the refrigerator as well as in cupboards to make back corners accessible.

Keep a stash of clean aprons in big and little people sizes so everyone who wants to join in food preparation can.

Create a cheery dining alcove in a small kitchen with banquette seating. Build plywood benches with hinged lids to store canned goods and seldom-used cooking equipment out of sight, but within easy reach. Top with fabric-covered cushions to add color and absorb sound.

If you have room, search out a large kitchen table to be used for informal meals and other activities. When you run out of counter space the table is a handy place to cool stacks of cookies, set up a buffet, or work on craft projects. A table with storage drawers for seldom-used cooking equipment or party supplies is a bonus.

Sink a decorative pottery bowl into a countertop to hold eggs and other items that tend to roll away. Consult a book on kitchen renovation for instructions.

Rather than hiding them in a drawer, store cooking utensils in a hefty bean pot, old crock, or pretty flowerpot.

Install a ceiling track-light fixture with moveable "cans" so you can spotlight the stove, sink, counters, and other work areas as needed.

Express yourself with sentiments that speak to you. A friend painted a Celtic blessing on the wall above our kitchen table:
"May you have warm words on a cold evening
A full moon on a dark night
And the road downhill all the way to your door."
   On nights when we're too distracted to come up with a personal grace we join hands and read that aloud.

Spices were once worth their weight in gold. They'll last longer if you don't place the spice rack above the stove where heat can rob their potency. Store spices in alphabetical order or group by category — baking, Italian, Indian, for instance — so you don't waste time rummaging for the right one.

Get a mortar and pestle. It's decorative and takes up less space than an electric grinder or food processor. Plus you'll have better control when crushing seeds and spices or bruising herbs. Shop for a heavy ceramic, iron, or marble mortar with tall, sloped sides.

You can never have too many pretty baskets. Collect them in different sizes and shapes to serve up everything from rolls to chips in style. Their woven texture makes a pleasing counterpoint to smooth china. Hang baskets from a beam or arrange them in the lost space between cupboard and ceiling.

Decant flavored oils, vinegars, and other condiments into decorative bottles and display them on the counter or windowsill. Pour scented hand lotion into an attractive cut-glass cruet and keep it by the sink.

The Dining Room

If you're blessed with a formal dining room, don't save it for the occasional "big deal" or holiday meal; use it regularly. Gather family or friends together for a relaxing repast on the weekend when there's time to get reacquainted after a week dashing about in different directions.

But what if you don't have a dining room? Anyplace with comfortable seating and a stable serving surface will do. One city friend, with a minuscule apartment, uses a beautiful wooden desk as both a writing surface and dining table. There's room for two to dine and when he has a party the desk serves as the sideboard for a bountiful buffet.

Setting the Scene

Unify mismatched chairs by painting them all the same color or adding cushions or slipcovers made from the same fabric. If you've inherited a full suite — matching chairs, table, and sideboard — and it's not your cup of tea, lighten things up by pickling the wood. One woman I know painted each chair in her grandmother's stodgy set as well as every drawer in the 1930s sideboard a different color.

When selecting tableware remember the rule of two out of three: if the china and silver are very elaborate the glassware should be simple. If the silver and glassware are simple, the china pattern can be more complex.

The Japanese say that we eat first with our eyes, then with our tongue, and finally with our hearts, but all cultures have understood that to dine well, food and drink by themselves are not enough. The spirit needs nourishment too. If the wine is sacred or even merely special, then so must be its glass. Don't wait for a holiday or other special occasion to use your nice things.

Always arrange furniture to make it easy to serve and clean up; keep doorways free.

Whether you're dining alone, with four, or with forty-four, tableware should be gathered and laid with as much care as is given the menu. The tabletop is as important as the clothes we wear — it's a personal statement about who we are. And, like our clothes, we change our tables to suit the mood, the season, the occasion.

Except for the most formal dinner parties, the only linens needed are napkins. While paper napkins might do for picnics, in my opinion they're too flimsy, skimpy, and rough for most occasions. It is more economical and better for the environment to buy and launder inexpensive cloth napkins that can last for years. Light-colored napkins are dramatic counterpoint to dark tablecloths (and vice versa). Repeated geometrics — checks, dots, stripes — make fantastic foils for florals, paisleys, and curvy prints.

Not all tablecloths must cover the table completely; smaller ones can be laid at angles with only their corners draping over the edges. Scarves, shawls, coverlets, runners, and other small fabrics can be laid atop large base cloths for an abundant, layered look.

Homing in on little details can make a big difference. Purchase small, inexpensive white bowls and use them to serve condiments such as ketchup, mustard, and jelly rather than plunking ugly supermarket jars on the table.

Anthropologists say that we gravitate toward round tables because they remind us of our cave-dwelling ancestors' communal fires. King Arthur's legendary Round Table helped eliminate quarrels among knights jockeying for position by making them equal, with no "head" of the table. A round table that seats six or eight is an ideal size for conversation. A square table doesn't have a head or a foot either, and like a circular one, is less formal than a rectangular or oval-shaped table.

Many cultures considered tables secular altars and to sit or sleep on one was looking for trouble. It was also bad luck to place new shoes on the table. Traditionally, Chinese tables were placed parallel to walls to encourage the uninhibited flow of positive energy. Food was passed clockwise, in the direction of the sun from whence all life came, to secure blessings. Salt, to protect both food and diners, was the first and last thing Romans placed on the table.

Paint your dining room a warm, welcoming pumpkin, red, burgundy, yellow, or bold blue to stimulate conversation.

When buying or updating casual and formal china, seek out compatible patterns to use as extra place settings for large gatherings. Mixing and matching (within the same formal or casual style) offers an imaginative way to revitalize old patterns. Mix different shades of a single color or combine solid-color plates with patterned ones in the same or complementary colors. Whites should be one tone, all warm (yellowish cast) or cool (pure white).

> *Be not forgetful to entertain strangers: for thereby some have entertained angels unawares.*
>
> — Hebrews, 13:2

Create a simple centerpiece by floating tea light candles and blossoms in a large, crystal-clear bowl of water. Or simply layer a glass wine cooler with whole kumquats and sliced lemons or limes, then wedge a tall taper into the fruit and ring with flower heads.

My Grandpa Nicholson always found a nice easy-listening or classical-music radio station to listen to during dinnertime. The television was turned off because it interfered with conversation that he felt was as important as the food on our plates.

Candlelight can magically transform any space. Plan on one candle per diner, arranged as either votive lights at each plate or massed together to make a centerpiece.

Giving Thanks

Take a minute to give thanks before or after the meal. Mealtimes are happier, and some say food tastes better, when the cook who prepared it and the source that provided it are acknowledged. You could say a traditional prayer or make one up to address the day's triumphs and concerns. A quote or poem would also work.

One holiday, humorist Mark Twain mailed cards wishing everyone a very Merry Christmas *except* the inventor of the telephone. Don't allow the telephone to disrupt your mealtimes; let the answering machine or voice mail pick up the call. Remember, the phone is there for *your* convenience, not that of the caller.

> *Think this over carefully:*
> *the most charming hours of our life*
> *are all connected — by a more or*
> *less tangible hyphen — with a*
> *memory of table.*
>
> — Pierre-Charles Monselet

The Living Room

The living room is usually the most important room in the house, furnished and decorated with the best we can afford. Some people reserve it for special occasions, with an imaginary velvet cord across the entryway. But does it really make sense to make the best and biggest room off-limits most of the time in order to preserve it for the relatively few times that we want to make a good impression?

Living rooms are meant to be lived in, not "saved for good." Furniture is more than decoration; it's meant to be used. After all, as author May Sarton once said, "A house that does not have one worn, comfy chair in it is soulless."

Live It Up!

Begin to create a user-friendly room by asking yourself what types of activities will take place in it. Will this room be used for playing or listening to music, watching TV, reading, bill paying, talking, or entertaining? You'll need a nook and a piece of furniture, perhaps multipurpose, for each activity. Will meals be served in one corner? Is there a view to be highlighted or disguised?

Open up small spaces with these popular decorator's tricks:

- Push back the room's borders by using shades of the same color for walls, curtains, carpet, and upholstery. Spice things up with throw pillows, vases, and other decorative accessories in bright or contrasting colors.
- Hang floor-length draperies starting several inches above the actual window frame.
- Polish the floors to reflect light and make the room appear more open.
- Look for a glass-topped coffee table or a wooden one with drawers to control clutter.
- Replace floor lamps with overhead or wall fixtures.
- Decorate with one large mirror, painting, or plant rather than lots of little ones.
- Confine your television and stereo equipment behind armoire or cabinet doors when not in use.
- Floor-to-ceiling built-in bookcases make the most of limited storage space.

Making the Most of Your Space

If there's no view, create a focal point with a favorite painting, poster, or collection. Or balance the bulk of a large armoire or the height of a tall bookcase with an arrangement of artwork punctuated by a mirror.

Furniture parked in stiff lines against the walls is inhospitable and makes a small room look even smaller. Soften corners and encourage conversation by arranging some large pieces at an angle. Use lighting, an area rug, or a large potted plant to anchor the grouping.

If you have space, select an overstuffed sofa big enough to seat three people with plenty of elbow room. One with a long seat cushion and removable back pillows doubles as a firm and comfortable spare bed. If you haven't room for a long sofa consider two love seats.

Drape a quilt or throw over the sofa arm for toasty toes and cozy catnaps.

Upholstered furniture carries more visual weight than other styles, so try to use these pieces on opposite sides of the room rather than clumped together at one end. Try mixing upholstered and wooden-framed or metal furniture for interest. The clean, hard lines of the metal or wood are a pleasing counterpoint to the soft, rounded upholstery shapes. Put casters on large pieces to make them easier to move for spring-cleaning or large get-togethers.

Combine floral or curved textile patterns with solids or geometrics such as stripes, checks, or plaids. Patterns similar in scale are the easiest to mix and match. If colors are in the same family (different shades of the same color, or all warm colors) and intensity you'll have the most flexibility.

HOMEY HINTS

Store candles in the freezer; they'll drip less when lit. Cup the candle's flame with your hand before blowing it out to prevent hot wax from splattering. Use a long piece of dry spaghetti to light tapers in hard-to-reach places. If wax has landed on your tablecloth or carpet, allow it to congeal, then scrape off as much as possible with a plastic credit card. Place a brown paper bag on the remaining wax and press the bag with a warm (not hot) iron, moving the bag as necessary until the grease is absorbed.

If you don't like busy patterns, use texture — twill, corduroy, brushed denim, leather — to create interest on upholstery, rugs, drapes, and other textiles. Dark or patterned upholstery is practical for pets and kids; newer fabrics have wipe-clean finishes. If necessary, protect soft furnishings with attractive, washable slipcovers or a colorful throw.

Add Tables for Function and Beauty

There should always be a stable surface within arm's reach to place a snack or pair of reading glasses. But coffee tables needn't be large or made of heavy wood to serve their purpose.

You'll also need end tables for lamps and the telephone. End tables needn't match, but they should have the same proportions.

Keep your eyes open; you might be inspired to craft a coffee table from an old wrought-iron gate, a grate, pair of shutters, or door. An oversize upholstered footstool works, too. Top it with a tray to serve snacks.

Benches are handy. They can visually anchor a wall of prints, and provide extra seating when you have a party. Our friend Eileen Murphy has a compact living room; she uses a narrow carpenter's bench as a coffee table. You can also use a bench as sideboard to serve snacks or as a table for little kids.

Decorative Accents

Personal collections turn a house into a home. Warm your place with things that have personality such as timeworn toys, old tools, or anything hand-crafted or painted. Stage a collection of conversation pieces. We kept a primitive xylophone on our coffee table for get-togethers and even bored teenagers found it irresistible.

But how to group all of those fabulous accessories you've accumulated? Find a common denominator. It might be a theme (birds or bells), shape, color, or texture (wire or straw). When I lived in a semi-furnished London apartment, trips to flea markets produced a decorative plate collection united by its blue-and-white color and cottage theme. I continued the theme with cottage prints and paintings as well as cottage-shaped tea cozies and teapots.

Craft a shadow-box still life with buttons, valentines, doilies, gloves, feathers, or anything you like to collect. Hang it on the wall or place it on a table.

Unify photos and prints by giving them all the same type of frame, or paint disparate frames the same color. Don't hang them higher than eye level, when standing, and group them together in one place rather than scattering them around the room. Prop photos on a strip of narrow molding for a more informal display.

What if there's no budget for art? Keep your eyes peeled when at the beach or on a hike for "found art" — shapely piece of driftwood, colorful shells, rocks, or bird's nests. Hang a bright quilt, scarf or shawl, inexpensive pottery plates, or heirloom family photos.

Edit your treasures. Not everything should or could be on display at the same time. There's a fine line between cozily cluttered and so busy that things are competing for attention. Rotate pieces or change accessories to salute the seasons.

A home should never be static; there's nothing worse than walking into a space and thinking, "This was done in 1972." Your life is constantly changing, and a comfortable home reflects that.

Don't hang delicate textiles, such as a piece of antique lace or cross-stitched sampler, opposite a window where direct sunlight could cause damage.

Break up rows of shelved books with framed photos and mementos, decorative baskets, bowls, or a statuette.

Seasonal Changes

Homes seem to take on a different feeling at different times of the year. We tend to retreat to the smaller cozy rooms during the winter and move into the open areas when the sun shines. Celebrate the change of seasons, especially if you live in an area where the temperature is the same most of the year.

Conjure up a mood change by decorating with different colors, patterns, and textures. Rotate paintings, prints, and other decorative accessories. Change lampshades and throw pillows. Give your sofa and armchairs a longer lease on life; buy an extra set of slipcovers in a seasonal color.

For a summer place, think cool, water-colored shades, lightweight fabrics, and floral prints or bold sunny colors. Pack away clutter. Roll up heavy wool carpets and replace with colorful cotton throws or enjoy the bare wood floors.

Warm, earthy colors and heavily textured or busy, patterned fabrics will psychologically take off the chill in wintry weather. Toss a nubby knitted throw on the sofa and the foot of your bed. Light lots of spicy- or balsam-scented candles.

Add Light and Color

Be bold. Paint a mural on one wall or, if you can't draw, make a collage or stencil a pattern to enliven your space. There are even new stencil kits that help you create damask designs on walls and floors. Matte paint subdues pattern; shiny paint enhances it.

If a room feels too small, light cool colors such as lilac, mauve, sea green, or dove gray will make the space seem larger. Paint ceiling and woodwork the same color.

Dark rooms can be lightened up with sunny shades in colors of golden yellow or spring green. Warm cold rooms by enclosing them with rich, hearty colors such as terra-cotta, old gold, and berry shades.

If you haven't the time or budget to paint a whole room, give the doors, window frames, and moldings a fresh coat, perhaps in a contrasting color. Wallpaper borders are a neat and easy way to add interest without investing much time or money.

You'll want soft mood lighting as well as bright, well-directed work lighting in every room. A good reading lamp by a cushiony armchair with a footstool is critical. Lamps needn't match. You might try sleek ceiling track lighting in addition to more traditional shapes. Three-way bulbs allow you to set the mood. Pink bulbs cast people in a flattering light; consider them if you're having a party.

Helpful Hints

Round out an awkward corner, hide a mess, create storage space, or block a draft with a folding screen. It can be made of padded fabric panels to complement your upholstery, or you could wallpaper or paint it to match the decor. You might even construct a screen out of old shutters.

Remove gum from carpets and upholstery by rubbing with an ice cube. When hard, simply pick off the gum.

Use a slice of white bread to wipe up broken glass shards. Bread slices can also be used to dust lampshades and wallpaper.

4

Private Lives
Bedrooms and Bathrooms

Give me, kind Heaven, a private station.

— John Gay

Each day begins and ends in the privacy of our personal chambers. We feel happiest in these intimate sleeping, cuddling, and bathing spaces when they perfectly reflect our personalities. Since most bed and bath areas are secluded rather than high-traffic spaces, your decorating druthers will be least compromised here. Feel free to surround yourself with colors and patterns that make you smile, essentials and not-so-essentials for your health and beauty rituals, and meaningful art and memoribilia.

A Personal Sanctuary

"And so to bed." Samuel Pepys, the famous seventeenth-century English diarist, always ended his entries with those soothing words. At the end of a long and busy day who doesn't long for his bed? The bedroom is our private retreat, a place to withdraw from the world, relax, and be recharged. We spend a third of our lives in our bedrooms. It's worth taking time to make yours a comforting, special place.

Selecting a Bed and Coverings

The bed is the most important piece of furniture in the bedroom, but once upon a time it was nothing more than a straw-filled sack laid on a bench or board. Handfuls of sweet-smelling herbs such as spearmint or pennyroyal were mixed with the straw to keep bedding fresh and repel fleas. A rosemary sprig placed under the bed was thought to prevent "evill dreames."

History aside, we expect the bed to give us a good night's rest, but it also plays a role as theater. The bed takes center stage; all other decorating decisions take their cue from it. Select wall, rug, and curtain colors after you've chosen your bedding.

An old superstition holds that bed sheets are imprinted with some of the sleeper's soul. People used to shake their sheets upon rising to prevent enemies from acquiring power over them.

Don't try to make the bedspread, curtains, and wallpaper match. It'll make you yawn! If the spread and curtains are patterned, keep the wallpaper simple. If the wallpaper is busy, go for textured rather than patterned spread and curtains.

Whether you prefer a sleek and sophisticated striped look, or a ruffled flowery bower heaped with lace-edged pillows, indulge your senses. Dress your bed with a variety of textures from soft cuddly chenille and prewashed cotton, to velvet and skin-soft satins for sweet dreams. You'll want different weights and colors for summer and winter. Even if the weather doesn't change all that much where you live, change your bedding with the seasons; it'll be a welcome psychological change.

Ancient Eastern wisdom suggests that you can spice up your love life with pink sheets and color consultants claim that the hue is nurturing and soothing. "Pink not only makes you feel good, it makes you feel better," says Leatrice Eiseman of the Pantone Color Institute.

Get creative with headboards. A wooden fireplace surround including the mantel, a folding screen, an iron gate, a grate, or simply draped fabric the width of your bed are all interesting alternatives. My Aunt Lois's "headboard" is a painted silhouette of grazing deer.

If it's too tiresome to make your bed every morning, invest in a duvet or comforter (they come in weights for every season) with changeable covers. All you have to do is give it a good shake.

Another bed-covering option is a quilt; they add homespun warmth and charm to any setting and their geometric patterns blend surprisingly well with contemporary furnishings. In *The Magical Household* Scott Cunningham asserts that there's magic in quilts. Interlocking and knot patterns as well as floral and herbal designs are considered auspicious; the Rising Sun pattern is said to be the luckiest of all. The first time you sleep under a new quilt or comforter pay attention to your dreams — they'll come true!

You'll probably want at least three pillows: one to sleep on, a firm one to prop yourself up for reading, and a squashy one to support your neck.

Rest Assured

Do you like the view from your bed? Would a decorative screen or large plant help to hide a dreary fire escape or cluttered desk? Place a favorite object, painting, or floral arrangement where you can see it first thing every morning. Display personal mementos, family photographs, and anything that you love or reminds you of being loved.

Invest in a good-quality, firm mattress topped with a pad. Turn the mattress top to bottom and front to back every couple of months and replace it, and the box spring, after ten years. Your back will thank you and you won't lose any beauty sleep. A foam egg-crate support mattress is particularly kind to arthritis sufferers.

Where is the best place to put the bed for a good night's sleep? The east is traditionally associated with spirituality and intelligence; some say the head placed in the east and the feet in the west prevents nightmares and aligns us with the power of the rising sun and moon. Others swear that sleepers whose heads face north, in alignment with the Earth's magnetic field, experience calm, riches, good health, and quick recovery from illness. Beware: Facing south or sleeping in a metal bed is rumored to invite insomnia and disease. Some believe that love, spirituality, creativity, and psychic abilities are yours if you place your bed facing west.

Feng shui practitioners think that the position of the bed relative to the door is more important than the bed's cardinal direction. The bed should not directly face a door, especially a bathroom door; the head should be against a wall or corner, not freestanding. Furthermore, don't hang a mirror on the wall opposite your bed; it could cause sleep problems.

Curtain Call

Create a closet by hanging a curtain behind the bedstead to store clothes.

Playwright Oscar Wilde's dying words were about his bedroom curtains: "Either they go or I do." To let in light but provide privacy, hang café curtains in two tiers, topped by a valance for eye appeal. A roller shade mounted behind the curtains shuts out extraneous light. Consult a book on window treatments for more specific insructions.

Lidded keepsake boxes, baskets, deorative hatboxes, wicker hampers, or vintage metal picnic baskets provide attractive storage in tight quarters.

HOMEY HINTS

Give your contemporary black-and-white photographs an heirloom look by soaking them in a strong solution of cold coffee. When the color is a little darker than you'd like, rinse the photos in fresh water and hang straight to drip-dry. You might want to test this effect on a non-favorite photo first.

Sticky drawers? Rub the sides of drawers with a bar of soap, a candle, or beeswax. If drawers still stick, sand lightly. This will also work on sticky window frames.

If noise is a problem, carpeting, shutters, or lined curtains will help absorb sound. Line the carpet with thick padding and choose the best-quality low pile you can afford.

Sweet Dreams

Dreams are mysterious, and every society has developed beliefs about their significance. Some thought that dreams were messages from powerful spirits. Egyptians paid careful attention to their dreams and wrote them down. The Bible records, in both the Old and New Testaments, many heaven-sent messages delivered in dreams.

The fragrances of herbs and flowers have long been known to encourage dreams. Craft a dream pillow, a small cloth bag filled with herbs that is tucked inside your pillowcase, to prompt dreaming. As you move your head during sleep, the herbs will be crushed slightly and release their fragrance. Consult Jim Long's *Making Herbal Dream Pillows* (Storey Books, 1998) for herbal recipes.

AN OUT-OF-BODY EXPERIENCE

Once upon a time, people believed that their souls left their bodies while they slept. Nyx, the Greek goddess of the night and mother of Hypnos, the god of sleep, tenderly guarded wandering souls until they were safely reunited with their owners.

Keep a notebook beside your bed to log your dreams as soon as you awaken.

What Else Do I Need?

Nightstands or end tables are practical places to pile books, arrange photos, and house a lamp, alarm clock, and telephone. They needn't match, but should relate to each other, or to some other piece of furniture in the room. A nightstand with a drawer or door is ideal for stowing necessities like eyeglasses, tissues, telephone books, paper, and pens.

If space is limited, install wall-mounted, swing-arm lamps on either side of your bed. Get three-way bulbs so you can adjust the light to your needs.

Place a lidded bench or chest at the foot of your bed to store out-of-season clothes or extra bedding. A child's chair or footstool can hold stacks of magazines or books.

A ceiling fan cuts down on the need for air-conditioning in the summer. Some provide for overhead lighting in the same fixture.

If there's room, include a comfortable upholstered chair, footstool, and small table to expand your sleeping space into a relaxing retreat for catching up on reading, writing, or just daydreaming.

If insomnia's not a problem, it's okay to have a TV in your bedroom, but position it where it won't be an eyesore yet can be viewed comfortably.

If your closets are small you'll need supplementary storage pieces. My husband fell in love with an old, pine sea captain's desk and uses it as his armoire. It has a pull-out shelf that we use to wrap presents or write letters, and he stows sweaters, T-shirts, and underwear on the shelves and socks in the cube holes labeled "bills" and "invoices."

Fresh blossoms in a vase, floral potpourri, and scented candles make your bedroom a sensual space.

Hook up bedroom speakers to the stereo system so you can travel from room to room without missing a beat.

Vanities don't have to be froufrou to function. One woman I know uses a chrome and glass Parsons table stacked with brushed aluminum, lidded boxes for cosmetics and jewelry. You might drape a hollow-core door (mounted on sawhorses) with a bright Indian print bedspread and hang a rattan frame mirror above it.

Tips for Organizing Closets

Other than some business suits, you'll put together more creative outfits if you hang all jackets, blouses, shirts, skirts, and slacks together by color rather than pair them as they came from the store.

Purge your closet of skimpy wire hangers — the dry cleaner will be glad to have them — and replace with plastic, wooden, or padded fabric ones to protect garments.

Other than shoe racks, try to keep everything off the floor.

How much stuff do you really need? Simplify! Go through closets, bookshelves, and drawers. Ask yourself, "When was the last time I used this?" or "Can I live without it?" Don't torment yourself with guilt; rest assured, in every closet lurks the skeleton of the unwise, wrong-size, icky-color purchase. Recycle clean, good-condition, unwanted items by donating them to a local shelter or Salvation Army thrift store. Every time you buy something new toss out two old things, whether they're magazines, gadgets, CDs, or clothes.

Lay out the next day's clothing and accessories the night before. You'll never discover that your shirt's missing a button on the morning of a meeting.

Mount a battery-operated light on the ceiling or wall of your closet.

Organize shelves with bins, stacking cubes, or see-through, lidded boxes. Store bulky clothing in plastic bedding bags.

Children's Rooms

Children's rooms need to be multifunctional with areas for playing, creating, sleeping, lounging, dressing, and studying. Bedrooms usually undergo at least three major transformations before kids leave home. Well-made, quality furniture flexible enough to serve children's needs at the toddler, "'tween," and teen stages is the most practical and economical in the long run. Here are some ideas for what to include in your child's bedroom.

Pine furniture can be contemporary or country in style, and there's no paint to flake.

In the beginning you'll need a changing unit; you could be changing diapers up to eight times a day. Choose a versatile piece, at a comfortable height, with a shelf and doors that can be used for storage later on. Simply add a changing mat to the top. Hang a wall shelf with pegs above the piece to store essentials or decorative accessories out of baby's reach.

When a child has outgrown a crib, purchase a regular bed — not a child's bed — that can be used for many years. If space is at a premium, a daybed with a pull-out trundle is practical for sleepovers.

When children share a room try to provide separate night tables or dressers and a shelf for each sibling. If they use the same closet, give each child hangers, pegs, and storage boxes in his or her favorite color.

Mount a decorative shelf over windows and doors or continue it around the room, for collections, stuffed toys, framed photographs, and artwork.

A metal trunk or footlocker can be used to store games, athletic gear, and out-of-season clothes. The top makes a wipeable snack surface as well as a place to play a game or put together a puzzle.

Recycle drawers from a broken dresser to use as under-bed storage.

No room for a desk? Attach a painted plywood half-moon shelf with a piano hinge to the wall; it can fold flat against the wall when not needed. Talk to consultants at your local home improvement store to find the right hardware.

Acknowledge children's individuality by letting them choose from paint colors and furnishings that you have preselected. They can select their own sheets; after all, they're covered up most of the time. When youngsters have outgrown the pattern, the sheets can be used as painter's drop cloths or picnic tablecloths.

Scrubbable painted walls are less trouble than fragile wallpaper in children's rooms; decorative wallpaper borders or stencils add definition.

Budding artists need an appropriate place to express themselves. When her children were small, my Aunt Lois wallpapered the lower half of each child's room with brown butcher paper. The kids were allowed to color with crayons on that portion of the wall. Another mother I know put up a chair rail molding and painted the space below it with blackboard paint (available at good hardware stores). The children were more than happy to cover the area with chalk doodles.

If you want children to hang up their clothes, provide storage with hooks and drawers they can reach. If space is tight, mount a coat or peg rack for backpacks and outdoor gear. Hang a monogrammed laundry bag on the back of the closet door; it can travel with kids to sleep-away camp and later to a college dorm room.

Every child deserves a personal bookcase or shelf stocked with a library of fantasy, reference, nature, nonsense, poetry, and stories. Books make great gifts for friends' and relatives' children, too.

Give kids a proper place, such as an oversize bulletin board, to display artwork, keepsakes, and invitations, as well as post photos, postcards, school papers, and reminder notes.

My Aunt Lois had a special box reserved for rainy days. In it were toys saved from the Christmas stockpile, old clothes and costume jewelry, and a piece of fabric ingeniously sewn in such a way that it could transform a card table into a playhouse complete with appliquéd shuttered windows.

Toys are more accessible stored in colorful plastic buckets; trash cans; stacking, see-through, lidded boxes; baskets; dishpans; or dresser drawers than they are in a large chest. Margarine tubs are ideal for housing small items. Use stick-on vinyl lettering (available from art-supply stores) to label containers. Mount Polaroid pictures on the front for preschoolers who can't yet read.

Furnish a young child's room with an adult-size rocker or cushioned armchair; you'll be more comfortable at story time.

Provide a tot-size table and chairs for tea parties, games, and craft projects.

> *A home is no home unless it contains food and fire for the mind as well as for the body.*
>
> — Sarah Margaret Fuller

Bathrooms

"From the water we made every living thing," reads the Koran. Our bodies are nearly 70 percent water so we're naturally drawn to the fluid that covers three-quarters of the Earth. Civilization always followed the flow of water that is vital for sustaining life, growing crops, and, in the days before superhighways, moving goods and travelers.

Paleolithic people discovered the healing powers of natural hot springs, and sanctuaries have been sited near springs and rivers ever since. Humans, in all cultures, associate "aqua pura" with creation, fertility, refreshment, and even rebirth. Purification rites are sacred to many religions; for Christians, a water baptism washes away sins. Muslims wash their hands before worship to restore purity.

Bathing Traditions

Our word for *lavender,* a cleansing herb, comes from the Latin *lavare* meaning "to wash"; before soap existed Romans bathed in lavender-scented water. Every town, regardless of size, had a public bathhouse where sociable citizens freshened up, ate, drank, exercised, gambled, gossiped, and conducted business.

Today, Scandinavians swear by the healthy benefits of a hot sauna trip followed by an invigorating roll in the snow or jump in the lake. The Japanese like to bathe communally, either outdoors in scenic mineral springs, or indoors in public hot tubs. Polite bathers wash before getting into the communal water.

Native American medicine men poured water on heated stones and employed smudges, smoking bundles of sweet-smelling herbs, in sweat-lodge purification ceremonies to enable the spirit to transcend the body. When Pocahontas landed in London, she was shocked to discover that, unlike her tribe, the English did not bathe daily. But contemporary English folk are said to use more soap than any other nation; they favor long soaks after a day maintaining a stiff upper lip. Americans, on the whole, are mad for a quick power shower.

Make Your Bathroom a Sanctuary

Perhaps you wake up standing under a steaming shower. Or maybe you prefer to shed the cares of the day as you sink deep into a fragrant tub. Either way, the bathroom should soothe, body and soul. It's meant to be an oasis, but it doesn't have to be luxurious for you to luxuriate in a world of your own. Here are some ways to make washing up a sybaritic experience.

According to Scott Cunningham's book *The Magical Household,* bathing in the morning increases beauty. Take a dip at noon or during a full moon for good luck. A bath just before sleep on Monday night ensures prophetic dreams, Tuesday's bath increases passion, Wednesday's boosts brain power. Bathe on Thursday to make money (especially if you toss a few silver coins in the water) and on Friday for romance. Saturday baths bestow patience and strengthen memory, Sunday's soak, good health.

A bathroom is not the best place to store or apply makeup; it's too humid. Better to create a grooming space in an alcove off the bath or set aside a spot in your bedroom. A lighted magnifying mirror will help you look your best.

A heated towel rack is a wonderful luxury found in cosmopolitan hotels. If you haven't got one, drape towels over a freestanding radiator or envelop a loved one in a towel straight out of the clothes drier.

To give to others we must first make ourselves whole. Replenish and recharge your energies by giving yourself a really luxurious bath. Assemble your favorite lotions and potions. Greta Breedlove's *The Herbal Home Spa* (Storey Books, 1998) is an excellent source of recipes for simple, all-natural body-care products.

Save old toothbrushes to scrub grout between tiles and intricate ornamental details on service pieces. Run the toothbrushes through the dishwasher or dunk in boiling water to clean before using.

There's nothing more depressing than a dark and dingy bathroom. Brighten yours with overhead track lighting or recessed can fixtures.

> *The maiden who,*
> *On the first of May,*
> *Goes to the fields*
> *At the break of day,*
> *And washes in dew*
> *From the hawthorn tree*
> *Shall ever afterwards*
> *Beautiful be.*
>
> — Old English Rhyme

Spa Style

If plain water seems a little, well, plain, add fragrant bubble bath, bath oil, or bath salts. Good-quality soap is one of life's best small pleasures. Next time you visit a specialty store look for bars made with fruit, tea leaves, or other unusual ingredients. Hard-milled soaps stored without their wrappers last longest.

Thick, soft, cotton towels are a must. Big or tall people appreciate extra-large bath sheets. Launder terry towels without fabric softener and they'll be more absorbent.

A thirsty terry-cloth or fleece bathrobe, at least one size too big, and comfortable slippers are wonderful to slip into after a relaxing bath.

An inflatable bath pillow with suction cup feet (the better to stick to your tub) will cradle your head and neck while you soak.

Pick up a metal, plastic, rattan, or wooden tub tray to hold your loofah, soap, sea sponges, and magazines.

Candles cast a golden glow over everything. Look for those scented with vanilla, chamomile, geranium, rose, jasmine, ylang-ylang, or lavender to help you unwind. Lemon, eucalyptus, rosemary, bergamot, or peppermint will pep you up. Orange blossom is said to impart a sense of peace and to ease jet lag.

A small, nonslip shower stool or built-in seat is handy. You can park your partner for a shampoo or sit to tend to your toes.

Hang up a DO NOT DISTURB sign, even if it's only in your mind.

Switch on the answering machine or take the phone off the hook.

Who says washing up has to be a chore? Toss into your tub a squeaky, bright yellow rubber duck or a flotilla of bobbing boats.

Play soothing instrumental music in the background (lyrics demand attention).

Bathroom Basics

Refurbish an old tub or sink by repainting the exterior and replacing the fixtures.

According to Mary Roses Quigg in *1001 Country Household Hints,* you can silence a drippy tap by tying a piece of string around the tap and allowing the tail to noiselessly siphon off the water (a temporary solution only — leaks waste precious water and should be fixed).

Glass shower doors make a small bathroom seem bigger. Maximize a small space by mirroring walls above tile, or use mirrors as a backsplash around sink or tub. It's a lot of drama for a little money.

Tile floors are easier to keep clean than carpeted ones. Wooden floors are practical if the floorboards are tightly laid, and the wood is coated with polyurethane (or painted first, then sealed with polyurethane). Add a runner, scatter, or area rug (with a nonskid backing) for color and barefoot comfort.

Embellish everyday towels by sewing on lace, ribbon, fabric appliqués, fringe, or other trim.

Steam and moisture take a toll on wallpaper; enamel paint requires less upkeep. You could make a big splash by using precut stamps and craft paints to simulate wallpaper. One art student I know stenciled a footprint frieze interspersed with the lyrics to "Splish, Splash, I Was Taking a Bath." What about a colony of frolicking frogs? You could paint a fanciful mural or simply sponge the walls a different color than the base coat.

Conventional decorating wisdom dictates painting a small space a light color to open it up, but it's fun to paint the bathroom a bold or crazy color that might be overpowering in a larger space.

All shades of blue, from turquoise to sea foam to cobalt, are ideal for bathrooms because of their natural association with water. Liven things up with warm-colored accents.

Unify your disparate pieces — mirror frame, cabinets, and cupboards — by painting them all the same color.

You can easily create a no-sew, designer shower curtain with a grommet kit from the hardware store and a king-size sheet. Follow the instructions on the kit and hang a plastic liner behind it.

Swap plain plastic shower curtain rings for glamorous shell-shaped or fleur-de-lis clips. You'll find decorative rings at bath supply shops.

Fashion a fabric skirt and attach it to the sink with Velcro strips to mask plumbing and provide storage.

Little things have big visual impact. Select attractive bath accessories such as tissue boxes, tumblers, soap dishes, and toothbrush holders. They needn't match but should complement each other. Replace harsh fluorescent lighting with frosted lightbulbs for soft, flattering light.

Hide clutter. Stash hair driers, shavers, and other appliances out of sight in a lidded container or behind a door. The same lazy Susans that organize kitchen cuboards can make toiletries more accessible in a small space.

To let the sun in and ensure privacy, install frosted, sandblasted, etched, or stained glass windows at eye level.

Patterned or lacy sheers also provide privacy without blocking natural light. You might prefer a snappy Roman shade or roller blind; install one that pulls from the bottom up. Craft nearly instant café curtains by hemming a channel on cotton kitchen hand towels and slide them on a tension rod.

You could screen a window with lush hanging plants. Or mount a thin piece of driftwood over a window and festoon it with a fishing net or piece of burlap. String seashells: simply pierce lightweight shells with a small drill and thread with knotted lengths of raffia or twine.

A narrow shelf running around the perimeter of the room is ideal for displaying decorative pieces such as perfume bottles, shells, folk art, and other collectibles. How about a playful gargoyle lurking on the shelf above the shower?

Brighten up a neutral bathroom with colorful accessories. Renew the room without a major overhaul by changing towel and rug colors with the seasons. New hardware makes a nice change — for small change — on cabinets and cupboards.

Try to arrange the room so that the toilet is not the first thing you see when the door is opened. Screen it, if possible, with a piece of furniture or plant. Feng shui experts recommend keeping the lid down and bathroom door shut so you don't flush away wealth.

Think creatively. For a small bathroom, roll towels into tubes and stand them on end in a big basket. Recycle a coatrack or ladder to hang robes or wet towels. An ornamental three-tiered pastry server could serve up scented soaps, and a toast rack could handle hand towels. Use a gravy boat, candy dish, or sugar sifter to dispense bath salts.

If you tend to run behind in the morning, make sure there's a clock in the bathroom to help you keep on track. A battery-powered waterproof radio allows you to catch up on the news in the morning or relax to music in the bath at night.

BATHROOM SAFETY TIPS

Forty percent of household injuries are due to falls. A water-absorbent bath mat with a rubberized bottom will reduce the danger of spills on slippery floors. Coir, bamboo, or wooden mats are also practical and attractive. Mount a grab bar in the shower and add textured appliqués to the tub floor to reduce the risk of slipping.

❧ 5 ❧

Home Run
Creating a Work Environment

Let all your things have their places. Let each part of your business have its time.

— Benjamin Franklin

Not so long ago, nearly everybody worked at home. For centuries merchants and artisans slept in or over the workshop. William Shakespeare's father was a successful glove maker, and his house included a workshop as well as private living quarters. Farmers always worked close to home; in medieval peasant cottages people cohabited with cows, pigs, and chickens to keep livestock secure and humans warm. In her book *Making a Living Without a Job,* Barbara Winter writes that until the Industrial Revolution, nine out of ten Americans worked for themselves at home. But after 1900, most folks moved off the farm and into factories and offices.

Setting Up a Home Office

Now we're living in the information age and technology has allowed an estimated forty million "lone rangers" to work successfully from home. Many people have started home-based cottage industries; others telecommute one or two days a week. Although you're likely to work harder and for longer hours at home, if you're excited about what you do you'll be more productive and it won't seem as stressful as slogging to some dreary office. Plus you'll get to spend more time with your family. There's a great deal of emotional satisfaction, as Winters says, in "making a life, not just a living."

Where Do I Begin?

Even if you're not interested in setting up a home-based business, odds are you'll bring work home from the office now and then. And everybody needs a place to pay bills, use the telephone, write letters, organize and store records, sort mail, and prepare packages for posting. Lighten the burden by assigning a permanent place to work where you can minimize distractions and spread papers out.

To create a satisfying spot tailored to your needs, start by examining your style. Is your ideal office all business, an efficient command center stripped down to essentials, or do you like a cluttered nook furnished with framed photos and plaques? Either way, the goal is to create an action-oriented workspace that feels at home with your home.

If you start small, but think big, office space isn't hard to come by. Stash a wooden lap desk, with lift-up lid, next to an armchair and a good lamp. Stock it with stationery, stamps, tape, scissors, and pens for when inspiration strikes or the dentist's office has put you on hold. Store files in a rolling cabinet at the back of a closet or disguised as a bedroom nightstand.

Convert a closet or recycle a seldom-used room into an office. As mentioned in chapter 2, you might find room under the stairs for a simple desk, chair, and file cabinet. A well-designed workstation consisting of a corner desk with pullout keyboard shelf would also make the most of a small spot. Set up shop in a corner or on a second-floor landing with a drop-front secretary and an occasional chair.

Don't buy equipment until you can't do without it. Many neighborhood stores now provide photocopy and fax services. The quality may not be top of the line, but it's a lot less expensive than buying a machine and supplies.

Open door policy? If you can't cope with frequent interruptions, do your best work in solitude, rely on lots of equipment or require heaps of storage for files and reference materials, create a dedicated retreat at the back of your home, in a basement, or on a top floor. Perhaps you own a large storage shed or garage that could be reworked.

A dual-purpose room is fine if you have one you don't use every day, have limited equipment and storage needs, or don't mind company around while you work. A shared space is most successful when you design the work area so that work can be packed up and put away at the end of the day.

Mount ceiling-hung blinds or install an accordion track divider, a folding screen, or other type of partition to carve out office space from the rest of a room. A tall, freestanding bookcase with adjustable open shelves and drawers could also serve as an attractive room divider.

Get Organized

If you're not naturally neat, you could mount rattan or canvas blinds on the front of shelving units to mask a mess. A wardrobe, armoire, or workstation with doors is also handy for hiding clutter. Install inexpensive industrial shelving along an entire wall and hide it with simple floor-length curtains.

If you've got a bigger budget, frame one window with a floor-to-ceiling, built-in bookcase. You'll need deep shelves for large reference books and binders. Craft long, low storage space under a deep windowsill. Float your desk in front if it doesn't block too much light.

A desktop organizer, document tray, and letter rack will keep papers tidy and conveniently close at hand. You could also mount metal magazine files on the wall. Personalize a store-bought cubby hole box; paint each drawer front with blackboard paint and chalk the name of the contents, or trace their outline, on the front. Press a plastic cutlery tray into service as a desk-drawer organizer.

Store old bills and records that won't be affected by heat, cold, or moisture, in the basement, attic, garage, or toolshed. If you've got a dust ruffle, under the bed works, too.

Check out the location of electrical sockets and telephone jacks before positioning your office furniture. Electrical equipment generates heat; make sure you have adequate ventilation.

Adequate lighting prevents eyestrain. Position your desk to make the most of natural light; add overhead lighting and an adjustable desk lamp with a three-way bulb.

Enhance Your Environment

Feng shui experts make these recommendations for a successful workplace:

- ↝ Avoid clutter. Organize your desktop neatly.
- ↝ Place a live, round-leafed plant or an aquarium with an odd number of fish in the far left (wealth) corner of the room.
- ↝ Suspend wind chimes in front of doors.
- ↝ Select a curved lamp and a wooden desk with rounded edges to promote the flow of chi.
- ↝ Position your desk as far away from the door as possible and on an angle or with its back against a wall for stability. If you can't face the door, put a mirror on your desk.
- ↝ Select a chair with a high back to help you climb farther up the ladder of success.
- ↝ Stimulate creativity by ringing a brass bell that you've fortuitously placed in the center right of your desk.

Here are some other tips for making your work environment both productive and attractive.

Simple window treatments such as blinds, shutters, or shades are easy on the eye and your pocketbook. Warm up a cold, slick surface — walls, furniture, equipment — with rough, rustic textures such as rattan, bamboo, and wood.

Paint walls a neutral color or a deep, rich shade like hunter green. Lighten up the latter with light-colored wooden, wicker, rattan, or metal furniture.

Create an inspiration corner. Hang up empowering quotes such as "Perseverance and audacity generally win" (Deluzy) or slogans, framed certificates, awards, or thank-you and congratulatory notes. My nursery school graduation form certifies that I was excellent at "stunts, hand work, and creative play." Every child in my class probably got the same rating, but on a bad day, it always reassures me that I am equal to the task at hand.

Use images for inspiration. A beautiful postcard or colorful print refreshes your spirit every time you

RECHARGE YOUR BATTERIES

Nobody can create in a vacuum. Designate at least one day a month (write it on your calendar) to recharge your creative batteries. During the Middle Ages, some Benedictine monasteries provided a garden and a bowling green for the novices to "re-create" themselves.

Do whatever it is that gives you a sense of pleasure, discovery, or excitement. Just for fun, take yourself out to the ball game, to the ballet, or for a bike ride on the boardwalk. Slurp an ice-cream soda for lunch. Get a pedicure and paint your nails purple. Sign up for carpentry classes or anything else you've always yearned to learn. Allow yourself to enjoy the process of acquiring a new skill — and scrupulously avoid grading the results.

look at it. A whimsical cartoon will coax a smile on a difficult day.

Studies indicate that listening to music by Mozart and Haydn will increase your creativity and productivity. Bach, Vivaldi, and Telemann are touted as focusing aids, but vocal music is considered a distraction.

Tips for a Healthy, Happy Workplace

There are many ways to make your home office both functional and comfortable. The key is to enhance the environment; satisfaction with your work and surroundings will naturally increase your productivity. For more tips on working at home, see Meredith Gould's *Working at Home* (Storey Books, 2000).

Spend a few minutes every morning organizing your thoughts and prioritizing your day before you dive in.

Noise pollution is an assault on our ears and nerves. Soften street sounds with a row of bushes that will act as a buffer between house and street. Apartment dwellers can muffle the sounds of their noisy neighbor's stereo by placing a full bookcase on the common wall.

Soften your office's hard edges with greenery. Leafy spider plants, feathery ferns, trailing philodendron, pothos, and dracaenae filter toxins from the air and release oxygen.

If your workspace is uncomfortably dry, an ultrasonic humidifier will replenish moisture and cut down on static electricity. Shop for one with features to minimize mold spores and clean it regularly, especially if you have allergies.

Clear your desktop and organize your life with a bulletin board. If you share your office with a pet that nibbles pushpins, place it well out of reach of your pet, or opt for a message board that uses strips of ribbon to secure notes and photos.

Perfection does not exist; to understand it is the triumph of human intelligence; to expect to possess it is the most dangerous kind of madness," said Alfred de Musset. There is a big difference between success and perfection. You'll get very little done if you insist on perfection, but can accomplish a lot if you focus on getting the job done.

Program yourself for success the way professional athletes do. Before a big game, they picture themselves sinking the basket or making a home run. Visualize yourself acing your presentation or landing a lucrative contact.

Only you can allow your time to be wasted. Be firm with long-winded callers; say that you've got a meeting coming up in a few minutes, even if it's only with your desk diary. When you haven't any more time to devote to a particular call, ask the caller if the comments or information could be e-mailed or faxed.

Divide all your tasks into Must Do, Should Do, and Like to Accomplish lists. Start with the Must Do list and cross items off as you tackle them.

It's said that when Martin Luther had too much to do he stopped to pray. If you're not religious, take ten minutes to sit quietly, close your eyes, and regulate your breathing.

> *One thing you can't recycle is*
> *wasted time.*
>
> — Anonymous

Sort mail next to a wastebasket. Don't be afraid to ditch unimportant communication unread. Slot correspondence into business and personal folders. Open the personal mail on your lunch hour or while waiting for the computer's printer to do its job. Save newsletters or trade magazines to read during downtime while waiting for a bus.

Save filing, tidying up, and other mundane tasks for the end of the day or at a time when your creative energies are at low ebb.

Switch to tea for your coffee break. Black tea is high in vitamins A, B, C, and E; the minerals fluoride, iron, manganese, magnesium, zinc, and potassium; and antioxidants. Tea also contains substances that lower blood pressure and cholesterol as well as stabilize blood sugar. A cup of black tea, brewed for five minutes, contains 60 percent less caffeine than a cup of black coffee. Plus, the caffeine is released over time rather than in one java jolt.

Work will never end if you allow projects and papers to migrate out of the office and into another room that serves another purpose. Assign everything a place and keep it there. At the end of the day, put everything away, or at least stack the papers into a neat pile, and switch off all machines. *Go home!*

> **We always have time enough, if we will but use it aright.**
>
> —Johann Wolfgang von Goethe

6

Home Away from Home

Temporary Quarters

Only that travelling is good which reveals to me the value of home, and enables me to enjoy it better.

— Henry David Thoreau

Creature comforts we take for granted in our own home are even more important when we're away from home. Whether you're on the road, temporarily living in a furnished flat, or hosting a guest, you'll want to make the experience as pleasant as possible.

Be My Guest!

Everyone loves to entertain the occasional guest, but often there's a lot of stress associated with preparing your home to welcome them. What can you do to make your shared time more pleasurable — for both of you?

Make a Welcoming Space

If there's a spare room in your home turn it into a restful guest room rather than use it as a dumping ground for out-of-season clothes, sports equipment, or furniture cast-offs. Guests are at your mercy; make them comfortable as well as welcome by anticipating their needs. Rest assured, you can warmly welcome your guests without a big budget.

Experiment with color, painting the guestroom a shade you've always wanted to try. If you don't have enough furniture, shop at auctions and yard and estate sales as well as do-it-yourself stores. Paint, stencil, stamp, or decoupage mismatched pieces to give them a unified look. If there's no closet add an armoire or an inexpensive canvas or wicker wardrobe. Trunks or a low chest of drawers provide storage while earning their keep as nightstands.

If you can't decide what size bed is the most practical, get two twins with identical headboards. You can push them together to form one king-size bed to comfortably sleep an adult couple. Check bedding catalogs for a special pad that fills the gap between the joined twins. Outfit both beds with matching skirts and shams as well as comforters in both twin and king sizes. Choose a tailored plaid or ticking stripe that looks crisp during the day, but dress the bed with pretty print linens and softly colored blankets.

> *Make your house fair as you are able. . . . Love the guest is on the way.*
>
> — Hymn, "People Look East"

Personalize the guestroom. Hang pretty pictures, a colorful collection of folk art (toy sheep for restless sleepers to count) or vintage and contemporary regional maps on the walls. An arrangement of stitched motto samplers would be cheery, and they're easy to find at yard sales and secondhand stores. Look for those that welcome guests with sentiments such as "May joy be with you / While you stay. / And peace attend you / On your way."

If you can't spare a permanent room for overnight company, outfit an office, study, bedroom of an out-of-state student, or family room for double duty. Transform a child's bedroom into an adult guest chamber with a change of lampshades and more sophisticated bed linens. Pack toys away in collapsible storage boxes under the bed.

A wooden sleigh bed, placed flush against a wall, can serve as both a sofa and a sleeping space. A daybed with a trundle tucked underneath can be made up as either a single or double bed.

Place the guest bed next to a side or end table, trunk, or low dresser, with a lamp; these pieces of furniture can work as a nightstand.

An armoire with hooks and shelves could house office supplies on one side and a guest's clothing on the other. If there's no closet, a standing coat-track takes up little space. Alternatively, shop the hardware store for a garment rack on casters that can be dismantled when not needed or for a door hinge that features fold-out hooks.

If space is really tight, buy a good-quality sofa bed for the living room. Look for an ottoman that opens up into a single bed, if both space and budget are limited. End tables can double as nightstands; clear off space to place a book, eyeglasses, and pocket change.

Move the coffee table and other furniture around so that guests can enter and exit the bed without stubbing their toes. Position a decorative folding screen to provide privacy and hide luggage.

During the day, hide bed linens in a sideboard, trunk, lidded basket, or footstool designed with storage inside.

Spend a night sleeping in the guest room or on the sofa bed to make sure the experience is as pleasant as your resources and creativity will allow.

If your guest room is used infrequently, leave time to air it out, launder musty linens, dust, and vacuum before visitors arrive. A separate guest bath is a boon, but if you haven't got one, make sure there's a place in the family bathroom or guest bedroom to hang a robe, wet towels, and spread out a toiletry kit. Put out a fresh roll of toilet paper and a new cake of soap. Make sure there's a shower cap even if you don't use one.

THE PERFECT HOSTESS

She makes you feel when you arrive
How good it is to be alive.
She promptly orders fresh-made tea
However late the hour may be.
She leads you to a comfy room
With fire ablaze and flowers abloom ...
What better way to please her guest?
The Perfect Hostess lets you rest.

— Elizabeth Paget

> **When there's room in the heart there's room in the house.**
>
> — Danish proverb

Thoughtful Touches

The mattress should be firm yet comfortable with no lumps, dips, or sprung springs. Insert a folding bedboard beneath the mattress if necessary.

Include one firm, one soft, and one baby pillow, enough for a person to prop himself up to read or watch TV in comfort. Make one of the three a nonallergenic pillow.

Make sure windows have shades or curtains that can be pulled for privacy or to shut out excess light.

An overhead light can be harsh and unpleasant; be sure to include a bedside reading lamp with a three-way bulb.

A radio makes a nice touch, especially if your guest has trouble sleeping. Most visitors will appreciate an alarm clock so they won't oversleep. And a teddy bear makes a comforting companion in a strange place.

Add some magazines and a couple of recycled paperback books for guests who may not have brought their own.

A glass water carafe and tumbler are elegant as well as thoughtful. A box of tissues and a waste-basket are a must.

If you won't be with your guest all during her stay, provide a spare set of house keys so she may come and go as she pleases.

Rustle up a bowl of hard candies or crisp apples for a midnight snack.

Make sure the guest will have access to a mirror; full length is ideal, but it should at least be big enough to see your torso.

It's a good idea to provide a flashlight for unexpected blackouts.

Visitors arrive with luggage. Clear out at least part of a closet, provide sturdy hangers, and a whole drawer so they can unpack clothes. Decide in advance where guests can stow their suitcases.

A small seasonal bouquet or flowering plant signals a warm welcome, especially if the guest room doubles as a home office.

A large, terrycloth spare bathrobe spans the seasons and will fit most guests.

How to Be a Gracious Host

Avoid last-minute scrambling; inquire if visitors have any food allergies or dietary restrictions. Ask what he or she likes to drink. Plan and shop for meals several days prior to a guest's arrival.

If your guest is an early riser or you'll be out the door before he or she awakens, arrange simple breakfast fixings — cold cereal, fruit, or muffins and instructions for how to operate the coffeemaker — on the kitchen counter. Unless you love to cook, make lunch a make-your-own-sandwich affair.

Prepare and freeze a seasonal soup or hearty stew ahead of time for dinner; when guests arrive you can spend your time with them rather than slaving away in the kitchen.

Call the chamber of commerce for free brochures on local attractions and up-coming events or check the newspaper for a list of what's doing. Suggest a couple of activities, but don't plan every moment.

Daydreaming in a hammock or dozing in front of the fire is a legitimate activity!

If you're not available to drive folks around, round up bus and train schedules. Provide first-time guests who are driving to your home with written instructions (include your phone number) and a simple map to follow once they have left a major highway.

Avoid hurt feelings. Be clear when you offer the invitation about when you would like guests to arrive and depart. Also, take the time to explain any house rules, such as "no smoking" or "please don't feed table scraps to the dog."

Advise visitors to bring special seasonal clothing such as snow boots or a sun hat, if it would make their visit more comfortable. Let guests know if you're planning any event for which they might like to pack something dressier than casual clothes.

What to Do When You're the Guest

"First day a guest, second day a guest, third day a pest." Have you ever heard this old proverb? Don't let it describe you; follow these suggestions to ensure a pleasant stay at someone else's home.

Don't wear out your welcome. Never complain and always be respectful of your host's house rules.

Prior to your visit, tactfully ask your host or hostess if there are any plans for your stay. If your arrival is going to be delayed, telephone your hosts.

Bring a little gift — a tasty tidbit such as a jar of gourmet popcorn or exotic salad dressing may be enjoyed by all or saved for later. Cut flowers can be a nuisance, because a vase will have to be found and they'll need to be arranged in water right away, but a no-fuss flowering potted plant is always welcome. Everyone can use a picture frame.

Always make your own bed and offer to help set or clear the table.

Send a brief thank-you note when you arrive safely home. If you took photos of your host's kids, pets, or garden, send them along, too.

Temporary Housing: Home Away from Home

It helps to think of the place you live as home even if it's not necessarily someplace you'll live for the rest of your life. If you've rented a beach house for the season or been posted abroad for a temporary work assignment, you probably won't want to spend a lot of money to redecorate or make radical changes. But there are a few tricks to make somebody else's place feel more like home.

Quick Fixes

If you've moved into a furnished apartment, rearrange the furniture to suit your needs. Perhaps the dining room would serve you better as an office and moving the table and chairs into a living-room corner would treat you to a view of the neighbor's rose garden.

If you can't replace or store unattractive furniture, change the accessories. Take down dreary paintings and prints and hide them under the bed or sofa. Pack up all the owners' tacky tchotchkes and replace them with things that tickle your fancy.

Lighten up dark, heavy drapes with a valance in a contrasting or complementary color. Or replace them with casual café curtains, plain white tab curtains, or rattan blinds. If the view's lovely, simply frame windows with a valance. You could create one in minutes by draping the curtain rod with a square lace tablecloth folded on the diagonal.

Check with the local library to see if they lend framed pictures or prints. If not, most museums and historic houses are rich sources for inexpensive posters. Artful postcards can be secured to lengths of ribbon with double-sided tape; top off with a separate bow and tack it to the wall. Shop for a wire picture holder with flexible arms of different heights to display snapshots and postcards.

Roll up dingy carpets and lay down bright throw rugs or sea grass matting. Cover less than wonderful wall-to-wall carpeting with area rugs or a runner. Big bold borders, patterns, or colors will make a large room look smaller; light colors, small patterns, or plain textured rugs will create the illusion of more space.

Consider buying new lampshades, a pretty glass pitcher (it'll serve up sangria and showcase daffodils with equal style), sheets, towels, and a shower curtain. Limit furniture purchases to lightweight occasional tables or chairs that can be shipped home when you're ready to leave.

Slipcover worn or ugly upholstery or drape it with a quilt, sheet, or colorful throw. Pile on decorative pillows in colors you like; vary sizes and shapes for the most impact.

Never underestimate the power of paint to transform a space. Walls usually need to be repainted when the previous tenant moves out. Ask if the landlord or leasing agent will let you choose the new colors.

Bouquets of fresh flowers, leafy hanging baskets, and potted plants contribute color and bring a breath of fresh air to a stale space.

My friend Eileen decorated her hallway with colorful paper, straw, and wooden fans. Another friend wired dozens of baskets to her living room's ceiling beam. Both collections were light enough to make shipping them home a breeze.

Select a Few Items from Home

I once saw a touching exhibit at Ellis Island of the things immigrants packed to help start life in an unfamiliar country far from home. There wasn't room for much in their small suitcases — a pair of candlesticks, a clock, a favorite book, an embroidered tablecloth, family photographs, and a tiny chess set — but even a few things can make a difference. Pack some portable items that would make a big difference — visually and emotionally — to you. Don't ask yourself what you need; rather, ask what can't you leave.

Rental kitchens are usually short on good cooking tools. If you're a serious cook, it's worth toting your favorite pan and best knives with you.

Keep a journal to record your adventures; it'll make fascinating reading for future generations. If jotting things down is not your style, collect postcards, save tickets, photos, and other memorabilia in an oversize envelope. You'll know where everything is when you're ready to sort it out and create a scrapbook.

Have a Happy Hotel Stay

The English word *travel* comes from a French word *travailler,* which translates as "to work hard." Travel is exciting, but it can also be a strain, especially if you're away on an extended business trip. Whether you travel a little or a lot these tips should help make your experience a positive one.

Choose your hotel room carefully. If you are traveling alone, request a room on an upper floor away from elevators, stairwells, and parking lots. Avoid vending machines, lobbies, bars, restaurants, and the street if you're sensitive to noise.

Always lock the door, attach the chain, and make sure you know how to find the nearest exit in case of an emergency. Hang the DO NOT DISTURB sign on the door to discourage intruders.

Feng shui expert David Daniel Kennedy suggests that you can travel safely by bringing a crystal ball and red ribbon to tack over your bed and a brass bell to hang from the room's doorknob. Protect personal chi by closing sink and tub drains as well as the bathroom door. Request a room where the hall door is visible from the bed.

Pick up a bunch of bright flowers from a curbside stand and arrange them in your room's ice bucket. The less powerful the scent, the longer they'll last.

By the time you've packed your clothes, you probably won't have room for a security blanket, but there's usually space for a token or two to remind you of home. Author Truman Capote always traveled with a collection of glass paperweights that he wrapped individually and separated like "quarreling siblings." I even know an executive who never leaves home without a framed photograph of her husband and their dog as well as a special teddy bear named Jemima. Because the bear was run over by a car, she's flat as a pancake and doesn't take up much room in her peripatetic owner's suitcase!

> *How long the years, how far I roam,*
> *I pray the path will lead me home.*
>
> — Anonymous

If the bedspread is truly hideous, turn it over or cover it with a blanket.

Fill the bathroom sink with warm water and add a few drops of your favorite essential oil. The familiar scent will permeate the hotel room, comforting you during your stay.

Bring a portable tape or CD player and a selection of tunes. Toss in a book on tape so your favorite author can read you a bedtime story.

Ask your significant other or a friend for a greeting card to tuck in your suitcase. Don't read it until you unpack at the other end. Prop it up where you can see it first thing in the morning and last thing at night.

Pack an immersion-coil water heater, a plastic mug, spoon, and packets of comfort food — gourmet tea bags, hot chocolate or dried soup mix, crackers, and cookies — in case you get the midnight munchies.

Pack a miniature flashlight in case of a power outage; check the batteries before you leave home.

If you've got a portable needlework project bring it along to help you unwind while you watch TV in your room after a long day.

Home for the Holidays?

As the song says, "there's no place like home for the holidays," but obligations might keep you far away from family and friends. Whatever the reason, don't wait for Christmas, Passover, or another holiday to arrive and discover that you have no place to go and no one to celebrate with. Plan in advance; maybe a family member or friend would like to combine a vacation with a visit to you. Invite someone, soon!

Perhaps you've lived in your new home such a short time that you don't know anybody or it doesn't yet feel like home. Look for other newcomers (at work, the gym, social or business clubs, church, or school) who might also be feeling at loose ends and invite them to your home. Even if they can't come, they might just invite you to a party at their place. If your kitchen is not fully operational, fake it. Buy pastries at a local bakery and invite folks over for coffee and dessert.

Flowers, candles, and scented potpourri are easy to find and contribute lots of holiday cheer. Travel treasures make wonderful souvenirs. Shop craft fairs, church bazaars, and street markets for hand-crafted or unusual table linens, menorahs, nativities, and other festive decorations.

You might not be able to find the ingredients to make some of your favorite festive foods. Children don't like change, and a traditional holiday is not the time to introduce foreign food. Ask someone from home to put together a care package and send it to you posthaste.

Before you leave home, pack an egg carton or padded envelope with some favorite Christmas ornaments; neither will take up much room in your suitcase. Stud oranges and lemons with cloves and display on a platter for a fragrant centerpiece.

Adventuresome adults might treat their taste buds to regional or seasonal specialties that simply aren't available anywhere else. You could discover something totally new or a new twist on an old favorite.

Use this holiday away from family and friends as a time for creative exploration. Ask yourself what aspects of the holiday mean the most to you. If it's cooking for a crowd, volunteer at a shelter to help prepare and serve a meal. There's nothing like helping somebody else to make yourself feel better.

Turn your back on tradition for a change! If you've always hosted a party, sign up for a guided tour or check yourself into a resort hotel with planned activities and a special holiday meal. Take advantage of the local climate, especially if it's different from what you're used to. Head to the beach for an exotic picnic or strap on a pair of skis for a cross-country trek.

If there's no room or time to set up a tree, keep Christmas the old way "bedecked with bayes and rosemary." Gather pots of green herbs on a mantelpiece or windowsill. Decorating with a bowl of hyacinths, narcissus, or other flowering bulbs is a Dutch custom and one you could easily manage with a trip to the neighborhood florist. Hang a wreath on your door. Candles always cast a cheery glow and "a bayberry candle burnt to the socket brings health to the house and wealth to the pocket."

Use large scarves or squares of colorful fabric to wrap gifts. Tied to the bedpost or a chair, they can stand in for traditional Christmas stockings.

CELEBRATING OVERSEAS

When you're in a foreign country, don't expect the locals to be aware of, much less celebrate, uniquely American holidays such as Thanksgiving. You could just skip the whole thing, but it's likely to leave you with a hollow feeling. Call the American embassy and ask if there are any events scheduled for the public. If not, request a list of American organizations (schools, clubs, and businesses) and call them to see if there are any activities planned. Be brave! Share a bit of your culture with acquaintances and new neighbors by inviting them to a good old American holiday held at your place.

Birthdays are personal holidays, or at least they ought to be. If you're away from home ask yourself, "What could I do here that I couldn't do at home?" Then do it. Maybe it's a formal afternoon tea at a posh hotel or a night out in a comedy club. Perhaps it's watching the sunrise over a boat basin and looking for manatees in the water at your feet. If you'd like a party but there's no one to throw it for you, invite a neighbor, coworker, or traveling companion to join you for a festive restaurant meal.

7

Inside Out

Window Boxes, Balconies, Decks, and Gardens

*What a desolate place would be a world
without flowers!
It would be a face without a smile,
a feast without a welcome . . .*

— Clara Balfour

Paintings and sculptures indicate that indoor gardening has been practiced since ancient days; Egyptians, Greeks, and Romans grew plants in pots. Wealthy people had elaborate terraced gardens, but even the poor indulged their love of flowers with a window box.

Plants and flowers make a home look cared for and welcoming. Contemporary studies confirm that people thrive in rooms filled with living greenery, but that's not news to students of the ancient practice of feng shui. They believe that the healing color of green actually enhances health, and that sick or dead plants drain your vital energy.

Hardy Houseplants

To bring any room to life, grace a windowsill, dot a desk corner, deck a hall, or round out an awkward corner with decorative greenery. There is a nearly limitless variety of plants to choose from, but base your choices on the indoor environment, the plant's climate and soil preferences, and the look you desire to create.

Feathery asparagus fern, Chinese evergreen, peace lily, trailing philodendron, and pothos are attractive and hardy houseplants. Succulents are easily grown indoors, too, and according to Scott Cunningham in *The Magical Household,* bestow love and abundance. African violets "promote peaceful vibrations" and Bird's Nest fern protects children and babies.

Leafy plants filter gases such as ammonia, benzene, and formaldehyde and release oxygen to improve indoor air quality. English ivy, spider plants, areca palm, lady palm, bamboo palm, Boston fern, and rubber plants will help reduce airborne pollutants.

If you pine for fresh flowers but the budget doesn't support regular deliveries from the florist there are a number of houseplants that bloom year-round. Brighten interiors with flowering maple, Cape primrose, New Guinea impatiens, fuchsias, lipstick plant, African violets, exacum, and Red Riding Hood mandevilla.

PET OWNERS BEWARE!

Several common plants are toxic to animals, especially cats; either don't include them in your home, or be sure they're kept well out of your pet's reach. Here is a list of some of the more common toxic plants: azaleas, bluebells, delphiniums, clematis, holly, lily of the valley, lupines, oleander, peace lily, philodendron (also toxic to children!), poinsettias, rhododendrons, umbrella tree, and yew. Your veterinarian or local nursery may be able to give you a more complete listing.

Cats eat greens to aid their digestion; provide them with their own pot of growing rye grass, oats, or catnip and they'll be more likely to leave your plants alone.

Brighten Your Hallway

If you're fortunate enough to have a hallway with a window you've got a good start, but if there's not enough natural light install a special plant light purchased at a hardware store or rotate greenery with plants from sunnier spots. Here are just a few ways to enliven interiors.

Bring cheer to gloomy hallways with plants that actually like low light such as an umbrella tree, rubber plant, and sansevieria. If your hall is drafty, move plants to a warmer spot opposite a window.

Gather groups of trailing plants on staircase landings where they can cascade out between spindles.

If all else fails, arrange masses of hydrangea blooms in a large vase without water. They'll dry beautifully and last for a long time.

Make a Fragrant Kitchen

Fresh, aromatic herbs taste so much better than dried ones; it's worth a little trouble to grow your own. Herbs generally prefer the outdoors because a kitchen can be too warm, but some are pretty tolerant. Try these easy-to-grow herbs:

- ⌁ Bay
- ⌁ Chives
- ⌁ Mint
- ⌁ Marjoram
- ⌁ Rosemary
- ⌁ Thyme

Place pots in a sunny window, mist them frequently with a fine spray, gently water once a week, and open your windows often. If possible, treat plants to the occasional day outside.

To decorate with other plants, plop ferns and spider plants on top of cupboards or hang in a window over the herbs. Ferns and spider plants like the kitchen's high humidity and will thrive if tended properly.

Enliven Your Dining Room

A table situated near a window, or a mirror amplifying the light from one, allows you to add to your dining pleasure with an arrangement of growing greenery. Place plants on the sill, in a free-standing window box, hang in windows in place of curtains, or in any other way that looks good and also appeals to you.

Eggcups (or hollowed eggshells placed in eggcups) would make charming diminutive vases for single blossoms; place one at each place setting.

> *I'd rather have roses on my table than diamonds on my neck.*
>
> — Emma Goldman

Try forcing bulbs — such as lily of the valley, hyacinth, or narcissus — to bloom indoors. A good nursery will have the materials and advice you'll need to start.

A vase of fresh wildflowers or an artistic arrangement of autumn leaves and trailing bittersweet make any meal special.

If you haven't already, start to build a container collection for flower arrangements. Patterned vases look best paired with flowers in the same tones; otherwise the design can overpower the arrangement. Check china cupboards, junk shops, and yard sales for anything that could hold water. A tureen, tankard, or teapot could serve up a spring bouquet. A cowboy boot lined with a jar would make a rustic vase. Glass never distracts from the flowers so all shapes should be considered.

HOMEY HINTS

Clematis, poppy, and hollyhock seem to droop almost as soon as you cut them. To preserve them, singe the cut end of each stem with a lit match to prevent their sap from draining away. Flowers arranged in water last longer when a sprig of foxglove is included.

Avoid placing floral arrangements next to fresh fruit; fruit gives off a gas that flowers don't like. Arrangements for the table should be either above or below eye level so diners can easily see and talk to each other.

Office Greenery

Plants soften and warm the functional furniture with which many offices are outfitted. A large tub filled with a tall sturdy plant, like a dracaena, grounded with an assortment of low or trailing greenery can function as a room divider and provide a measure of privacy.

A window full of hanging plants is a pleasant spot to rest tired eyes after staring at a computer monitor. A shallow dish planted with a sculptural bonsai tree doesn't take up much room and makes an artful display.

If your office has good light, you could fill a low, wide bowl with cacti, succulents, and jagged rocks to make a desktop desertscape.

Blossoms for the Bed & Bath

If you can't find anyone to water your plants while you're out of town, line the tub with a large bath towel and fill with a few inches of water. Place potted plants on the towel so they can water themselves.

We'd love your thoughts . . .

Your reactions, criticisms, things you did or didn't like about this Storey Book. Please use space below (or write a letter if you'd prefer — even send photos!) telling how you've made use of the information . . . how you've put it to work . . . the more details the better!

Thanks in advance for your help in building our library of good Storey Books.

Pamela B. Art

Publisher, Storey Books

Book Title: _____

Purchased From: _____

Comments: _____

_____

_____

_____

_____

Your Name: _____

Mailing Address: _____

E-mail Address: _____

☐ Please check here if you'd like our latest Storey's Books for Country Living Catalog.

☐ You have my permission to quote from my comments and use these quotations in ads, brochures, mail, and other promotions used to market Storey Books.

Signed _____ Date _____

e-mail=feedback@storey.com   www.storey.com   PRINTED IN THE USA   4/99

From: _____

BUSINESS REPLY MAIL

FIRST-CLASS MAIL   PERMIT NO. 2   POWNAL   VT

POSTAGE WILL BE PAID BY ADDRESSEE

STOREY'S BOOKS FOR COUNTRY LIVING
STOREY COMMUNICATIONS INC
RR1 BOX 105
POWNAL   VT   05261-9988

NO POSTAGE
NECESSARY
IF MAILED
IN THE
UNITED STATES

Cyclamen is said to safeguard sleepers, and a weeping fig bestows a good night's sleep. Hook baskets of trailing plants on a sturdy curtain rod over a window or dangle them from decorative wall brackets.

Soften a sharp-edged bookcase with cascading ivy; use potted African violets as bookends.

Spider plants, philodendrons, and ferns love humid bathrooms, hang them in windows in place of curtains.

Cluster other moisture-loving plants on a windowsill, counter, on top of the medicine chest, or on a ledge above the shower.

Roses symbolize beauty and grace. A bud vase filled with sweetly scented stock and miniature roses would invite sweet dreams and welcome the morning.

Container Gardening

Have you ever walked past a row of anonymous, look-alike apartment buildings and noticed the burst of color contributed by just one little window box brimming with blossoms? Gardening in a container or in a confined space, such as your balcony, terrace, or patio, doesn't have to be second best for those without access to a yard.

Frame Your View with Window Boxes

The earliest windows (from the Old English "wind's eye") were mere slits to let air in and smoke out. Until the seventeenth century, only the wealthy could afford glass, and that was in the form of small, blurry, or entirely opaque panes; less prosperous folks had to make do with oiled paper. Celebrate your clarity of vision by framing your view with foliage or floral window boxes; they'll give as much pleasure looked at from the inside as from the outside. And on a drizzly day you can garden without ever getting your feet wet.

Window boxes and traditional houses go together like a horse and carriage, but they can add personality and warmth to contemporary designs, too. Choose a box style and plants to match your home's design.

In *The Windowbox Book* Diana Stewart suggests that you lay a piece of tissue paper over a photo of the front of your house and sketch in several decorative combinations, including shrubs, hanging baskets, and ground-level planters, to gauge the total effect before you rush out to the garden center to purchase containers.

Buy or build window boxes that are at least six inches deep, recommends Marianne Binetti in *Shortcuts for Accenting Your Garden* (Storey Books, 1993). Line boxes with Styrofoam peanuts or broken crockery (curved side down) for drainage and place blooming plants, pot and all, right in the box. Hide the pot rims with bark chips or moss.

Although conventional wisdom suggests that boxes should be as wide as your windows and as deep as the sill, you might discover that it is more attractive to mount wider boxes below the sill, especially if ledges are very narrow.

Consider hanging balcony boxes inside the railing. For safety's sake, support boxes with brackets or secure with chains. A heavy terra-cotta or reconstituted stone box should be permanently secured so there's no chance of injury to neighbors or their property.

Frame window boxes with a pair of hanging baskets on decorative brackets to maximize the effect.

Thin plastic window boxes are inexpensive, but might buckle when filled with heavy soil or crack after prolonged exposure to sun. Fiberglass is a better bet and won't need watering as often as wooden boxes. Window boxes made with rot-resistant wood — ash, cedar, oak, or redwood — are more expensive, but won't rot as quickly as those made from softer materials, nor do they require paint or varnish. You may choose to stain or paint window boxes to coordinate with or complement the color of your door, shutters, and other trim, however.

From the Ground Up

If there's no room underfoot, look up. Take advantage of a sunny wall to create a vertical garden. Anchor halfpots directly to the wall or slip pots into mounted metal racks. Break up the vertical arrangement with hanging buckets or baskets swinging from decorative wall brackets.

Rig up a wall-mounted fountain to enjoy the soothing sound of splashing water.

Hanging baskets are truly beautiful when crafted correctly. It's less trouble to use a plastic basket with an attached drip tray, but it won't look as pretty as a wire basket filled with moss. Aim for an interesting mix of foliage and flowers; avoid flowers with the same shape and size, or those with similar leaves. Place the tallest, biggest, or most colorful plant dead center as a focal point. Some favorite basket plants are pelargoniums, cornflowers, daisies, fuchsias, begonias, impatiens, morning glories, stocks, asters, alyssums, geraniums, and busy lizzie.

If you support the stems with the help of a firmly grounded wire grid or wooden trellis, you can even grow old-fashioned cottage garden flowers like hollyhocks or sunflowers. Ask experts at the local hardware or garden shop for advice about the type of hardware best suited to your wall's surface so you won't have to wander the neighborhood hunting your trellis after a bad storm.

Transform a Balcony or Terrace

If you live in an apartment you can create a container garden on a balcony or terrace. Decorative tubs, boxes, bowls, barrels, milk cans, jardinieres, crocks, or urns can help transform a bleak concrete space into a lush oasis.

Junk shops and scrap yards are good sources for unusual containers. An old watering can, coal scuttle, bucket, toy wagon, or wheelbarrow would be an interesting variation, but be sure to drill a drainage hole in the bottom of any container that doesn't have one.

Small, delicate flowers whose charming details might be overlooked in a large garden will come into their own on a balcony or terrace. Cultivate a mixture of low-growing, tall, hanging, and climbing plants. Colorful climbers such as clematis, honeysuckle, jasmine, passionflowers, and morning glory will offer shade, provide privacy, and act as a windscreen.

Vary the size and shape of containers for maximum interest, but don't allow the container's color or decoration to overshadow the plant. Think of a container as a picture frame rather than the picture. Terra-cotta pots suit traditional and country looks; metal and translucent frosted pots look at home in contemporary settings. Group odd numbers of smaller pots together for visual impact rather than scattering them about.

Prop wooden planters up on bricks or risers to promote air circulation and prevent bottoms from rotting.

In a hot, sunny climate plant your garden in cool colors — heavenly shades of blue, delicate lilac and mauve, deep purple, and bright white with green and silvery green foliage. Warm up cold, gray, concrete quarters with bright sunny yellow, bold orange, robust red, rust, and yellow-green flowers and plants. Complementary colors, such as blue and orange or red and green planted next to each provide lively focal points.

Marianne Binetti makes this creative suggestion in her book *Shortcuts for Accenting Your Garden* (Storey Books, 1993): If you don't have enough floor space, include a trio of hanging pots. "By hanging three pots one right under the other (or one hanging from the bottom of the other), you create a pyramid of plants but have to water only the top one. Let the water flow out of its drainage holes and into the plants below."

Large containers won't need to be watered as often as little ones, but their weight might be a problem. Check to make sure your balcony can safely support them. Attach rolling casters to the bottom of unwieldy pots or place them on a wheeled platform.

Include scented geranium, alyssum, dianthus, sweet peas, lavender, lemon verbena, or other plants with a pleasing scent to leave a sweet impression on your clothes and hair as you brush by.

Remember that plants potted in containers will dry out much more quickly than those bedded in the earth. When it's hot, dry, or windy, plants will need to be watered at least once and perhaps as many as three times a day. Provide every container with a saucer so water doesn't run down the balcony and splatter your downstairs neighbor's patio.

Enhance Your Patio with Color and Shape

It's easy to blur the line between indoors and out if you think of your plain patio or deck as an outdoor living room. Here's an old trick: If your sofa and armchairs are upholstered with a floral pattern, plant the same types and colors of flowers on the patio to visually stretch the living room. If your style is more restrained, position potted palms or tall sculptural cacti (light from underneath with can lights) in a corner near the door to the deck and place more of the same type specimens outside.

Be sure to include a table for serving snacks or spreading out a craft project. Give an old picnic table a new lease on life by painting the top to look like a wrinkled red and white checked tablecloth and, just for fun, write "just add ants" with a felt-tip marker.

Every patio or deck needs a rocking chair, porch swing, or hammock to encourage loitering. If there's room, consider a wrought-iron baker's rack, rattan etagere, or corner shelves to house plants and other decorative objects.

> *If you would be happy for a week, take a wife; if you would be happy for a month, kill a pig; but if you would be happy all your life, plant a garden.*
>
> — Chinese proverb

Does Monday morning make you grimace? Breakfast alfresco at a patio table decorated with a floral centerpiece rather than indoors behind the kitchen table.

Outdoor Paradise

Garden is the Persian word for paradise. If you're blessed with a garden, live in it — don't just landscape it. Treat your garden as an extension of your house by creating a series of outdoor rooms for different moods and activities.

Identify the best location to enjoy your morning cup of coffee, shelter in the dappled shade, or soak up a spectacular sunset. Use bent-willow walls, bamboo dividers, or graceful ornamental grasses that rustle in the breeze to screen off one area from another.

Appeal to your sense of smell with a scented lavender border (a bonus: its fragrance keeps pests at bay) or rosemary topiary. Closely cropped chamomile or thyme makes a fragrant walking path; plant the herbs in spaces between paving stones.

Garden ornaments are especially important in winter when there might not be much else to look at. Inject a little color into gray winter gardens by painting tubs, benches, gates, and trellises a bold blue or bottle green.

A graceful arch, gate, or trellis smothered in scented flowers would add height to your landscape, provide shade, and gracefully usher you into a tranquil spot set aside for relaxation. Use tree branches to support rambler roses or attractive parasites such as mistletoe. Furnish your tranquil sitting room with a cushioned bench or hammock overlooking a vista punctuated by a decorative focal point.

MAKE A LITTLE MAGIC

Some enchanted evening, when the weather is obliging, set up a proper table with a floral-sprigged cloth (anchor the corners with decorative crocodile clip weights) and comfortable cushioned chairs out on the lawn under a canopy of spreading trees. If the trees aren't yet big enough erect a giant flower-crowned garden umbrella. Shift a pair of upholstered armchairs from the living room to hold court at the head and foot of the table.

Hang softly glowing lanterns in the trees or festoon trunks (and branches, gates, arbors, and fences) with strings of twinkling Christmas lights. Line walkways with lighted candles anchored in sand-filled paper bags, and dot leaf-wrapped votive candles at every place setting. Create a similar table setting indoors, round out bare corners with tubs of greenery and flowers, and let the party float seamlessly between these two dining rooms.

Define an alfresco dining room by laying a decorative tile or rustic brick "rug" in a herringbone or basket-weave pattern.

Create a proper place for kids to play away from flowers and fragile garden ornaments. Create a temporary playroom by erecting a tepee, tent, or canopy made from a sheet. Plant fluttering banners or windsocks on poles to stake out a special place to celebrate a birthday party.

A scarecrow placed at the end of winding path adds a whimsical touch. Or make a maze, in a small space, using miniature shrubs.

Abstract sculpture suits contemporary gardens; a sundial or architectural relic would complement a more traditional one. A bubbling fountain is lovely to look at, and the splash of the water can be hypnotic. Feng shui experts favor birdbaths that attract good chi and birds that replenish energy.

> *Summer afternoon — summer afternoon; to me those have always been the two most beautiful words in the English language.*
>
> — Edith Wharton

An herbal knot garden would contribute architectural interest as well as ingredients for the soup pot or potpourri.

Gardens naturally attract critters, some of which have been revered since ancient times as good omens. They say that if a bee flies in your window you'll hear good news; a ladybug landing on you will lift your sorrows when she flies away. Spiders were thought to protect the house and it was unlucky to kill one. Frogs attract rain as well as new friends. Touching a turtle's shell is supposed to bring good luck. A cricket chirping on the hearth is a symbol of a happy household, but if it leaves, watch out! If your garden is confined to a high-rise balcony you might attract some good vibrations with a carved stone cricket.

8

Moving Out and Moving On

*'Tis here they say the journey ends
And little doubt it must be so
But, as I tell my bestest friends,
I hate to go.*

— Eden Phillpots

Accurding to the U.S. Postal Service, the average American moves about twelve times during his or her life. Military personnel, diplomats, corporate global nomads, and expatriates and their families may move as often as every two or three years.

Moving is an exciting adventure as well as an opportunity for a fresh start. But every move, even just across town, is a trip into the unknown.

Leaving behind people and places interrupts friendships and continuity. Human beings don't like change. Dr. Jill Kristal, psychologist with the American Counseling Center in London, ranks the stress of moving one level below stress resulting from the death of a loved one, a divorce, or incarceration.

If you're about to be up-rooted or have just been planted in a new place this chapter will help you bloom again.

So Long, Farewell

According to Dr. Kristal, the most important way to prepare yourself for a move is to say a proper good-bye. Most people avoid a formal leave-taking because they find it awkward and sad. It's easier to lose yourself in the packing than cope with the emotions that come up when you tell family and friends good-bye. Nevertheless, without a clean ending there's little chance of a fresh start.

Saying Good-bye to Friends

Say good-bye to your home and neighborhood as well as your friends. Take a last walk around your old haunts — the park, grocery store, corner café.

Plan a special last time with closest friends and family a few weeks before the movers arrive. Get all your feelings out on the table.

Begin by telling people about the move as soon as you have a firm date. Everybody will need time to get used to the idea. Kids are likely to be shocked, scared, angry, and sad. Adults might be excited for you and jealous at the same time. No matter how painful, try to maintain your relationships to the last moment.

Throw a party and invite family and friends to speed you on your way by signing a bon voyage tablecloth you can take with you. Kids might prefer a T-shirt or baseball cap. Take plenty of photographs and put them in a small album to pack in your open-me-first box. Have a new address book on hand for family and friends to fill in. If possible, give guests prestamped blank postcards or envelopes with your new street and e-mail address.

> *Honor the house in which you were born, the tree that gave you shade, and the village where you were raised.*
>
> — Swedish proverb

Parting with Your Favorite Places

After everything's been packed up walk through each room and try to remember one special thing that happened there. Psychologists say it's helpful for kids to see the house stripped bare so they'll know that there's no turning back. Give children a piece of chalk to scrawl a message, trace their hands or draw a picture on the bare walls of their old bedroom.

If you have a fireplace, take a small piece of wood with you to light a fresh fire in your new home.

Tips for a Smooth Move

There are several old superstitions concerning moving. Don't move on a Friday. Don't take your pig trough. Don't take your cat unless you make it wave good-bye to your neighbors. Don't take an old broom to a new house. But you might like to make a clean break by ceremoniously sweeping yourself to (not out — that's bad luck) the door with it.

These quaint superstitions might not seem applicable to you, but what *should* you do if you're planning to relocate?

Familiarize yourself with your future home as much as possible before you take leave of your current home.

Tell everyone you know where you're going and ask if they know anyone there. If they do, see if they would be willing to give you that person's name, phone number, and address. If you belong to a club or professional organization ask them if they have a list of members in your home-to-be.

Contact the local chamber of commerce or tourist board to request a list of newcomer's organizations, special interest groups and social clubs, libraries, parks, places of worship, schools, and professional organizations. Request brochures on local attractions and special events as well as maps.

Subscribe to your new local newspaper and have it sent to you at your current address. This way, you'll have a leg up on where to go and what to do as well as local politics and key players.

Contact your college alumni department to see if there's anybody from your old school living in your soon-to-be home. It doesn't matter if there's a big age difference; you've got two things in common: your alma mater and the new town. Write to the person a month before you're due to arrive to see if you can make a date to meet.

Lighten Your Load

You can lighten your load and considerably reduce costs by editing belongings before, not after, your move. As soon as you've fixed the moving date start sifting through your things. Be ruthless!

When you've finally got everything sorted, take out a newspaper ad, hold a yard sale, or make a donation to charity. Some charities will even pick up household items and give you a receipt. Let older kids run their own garage sale and keep the cash.

If you haven't worn it in over a year, never liked it (even if your mother gave it to you), or it won't work in your new home, don't pack it.

Pick a room per week and go through it with a pile of large plastic garbage bags labeled "keep," "sell," "throw out," and "give away." Start with the least meaningful items. If you're not sure whether or not to ditch something, put it in the "throw out" bag and give yourself an hour before you can retrieve it. Odds are you won't.

Work with young children to decide which toys and books to sell or give away. Explain that this is an important step in making room for new things in the new home. Suggest that they give outgrown clothing and toys they no long play with to other kids who don't have as much. Resist the urge to "help" kids by throwing things away for them; it will only make them feel more out of control. Sometimes the threadbare bear that's been sitting on the shelf for months may be needed again to help your child cope with the turmoil of the move.

Get Ready

Pick up free change-of-address cards at the post office and fill out an official change of address form. Enlist the entire family's help in completing and mailing cards to everyone who will need your new address — family, friends, banks, credit card companies, doctors, schools, and others.

Measure the windows, doors, and rooms in your new home to make a rough floor plan. Check to see what curtains, rugs, and furniture will best fit each room and mark it on the floor plan. Make an extra copy for the movers and give it to them the day of the move.

If no one's thrown you a good-bye party, host one for yourself. Keep it simple; make it potluck, a pizza party, or cake-and-coffee affair.

EMERGENCY ESSENTIALS

Pack an open-me-first box or suitcase with essentials in case you arrive before the moving van. After it is packed, label the box DO NOT REMOVE and put it in the car yourself. Include in your open-me-first box: bathroom necessities such as medication, bandages, shampoo, toothbrushes, and toothpaste; kitchen helpers such as plastic or paper plates, and cups, a roll of paper towels, a bottle of all-purpose cleaner, and pet food and dishes (and litter box), if applicable; general items such as keys, checkbook, personal address book, lightbulbs, pad and pencil, and a battery-powered clock radio; basic tool kit, packed with items such as a flashlight with batteries, metal tape measure, screwdrivers (regular and Phillips head), hammer, nails, and pocket- or utility knife.

Karen Zinkowski of Suffolk, New York, suggests that you pack copies of telephone directories, both white and yellow pages; you'll have the address and phone numbers of friends and businesses "back home." Make your first stop in a new town some place that you can pick up a street map and a copy of the yellow pages.

Pack fine jewelry yourself, as well as a suitcase for each family member with a week's worth of clothes.

Ask your vet for advice on moving pets safely.

Let each child pack a backpack with a snack, a book, and a toy or game that can be played in the car or on the plane. (Do check to make sure there's nothing inside that the airlines wouldn't like on board.)

Moving In

While there's no doubt that moving into a new home is exciting, it is also time consuming and tiring. To make your unpacking as painless as possible, try the following ideas.

Set up and make the beds. My cousin Eileen suggests taking a nice hot shower, turning off the lights (so you can't see the mess), and snuggling in bed with someone you love.

Clean the bathroom and unpack your bathroom essentials. Clean and organize the refrigerator and food preparation area in the kitchen. Sweep, wash, or vacuum floors, drawers, and cupboards before unpacking.

Create a box-free relaxation zone even if it's nothing more than a rug, radio, lamp, and pile of pillows. At the end of the first day sit down with a refreshing drink and take a deep breath. If you can find photos of family and friends get them out and take a few minutes to remind yourself that your loved ones are with you in spirit.

Connie Anderson of San Marco, California, says that after the movers left, her mother always said, "We can't go to bed without something green and living in this house." She'd make huge bouquets from any shrubbery she could find in the yard for the top of the piano, at the head of the stairs, and for each person's dresser.

Settling Down

Even though you might not feel like it, force yourself to reach out and explore your new community. Holing up at home will only make you feel more isolated. Initiate conversations; offer a coworker or new neighbor a cup of coffee. Accept every invitation. Join a social organization or gym even if you'd never do that back home.

Scan bulletin boards at the library, church, synagogue, copy center, grocery store, and laundromat for information about local activities from hiking clubs to clean-up day in the neighborhood park. Sign up for a class in something you've always wanted to try. Tell yourself that you do have friends in your new home, you just don't know their names yet.

Find new ways to have fun. Ask kids to take you on a new ride at an amusement park. Search out a student film festival at a local university. Visit an ethnic restaurant and order something you've never tasted.

Allow yourself little treats. Buy a bunch of bright flowers or drop off the laundry. It may lighten your bank balance, but it'll save your sanity.

Relocating to a Foreign Country

In addition to all the normal activities associated with relocation, moving to another country has its own set of concerns. First, experts suggest that you keep your home or apartment if at all possible because it makes repatriation easier. You might try to rent it out, either furnished or unfurnished. Be sure to make a household inventory for insurance purposes. A video or photos of every room in the house is a good way to start.

Before You Go

Ensure that your passport is valid. Get extra photos and start paperwork for a visa and driver's license.

The Department of Agriculture should be able to provide information about importing pets. Ask if there is a quarantine and what immunizations and paperwork are required.

Contact the U.S. Department of Health and ask what shots are recommended for the country where you are moving. Make appointments with doctors and dentists for check-ups and vaccinations. Obtain copies of prescriptions for glasses, contact lenses, and maintenance medications. Ask if there are alternatives sold overseas.

Get copies of all medical, legal, and insurance records. Update wills if necessary. Request a letter from your auto insurer affirming your good driving record.

Try to set up a visit to look for schools and housing before you move. Ask for a list of local doctors, dentists, schools, social clubs and professional organizations, places of worship, and tax consultants. Request local maps.

> *Shall I abandon, O King of Mysteries, the soft comforts of home? Shall I turn my back on my native land, and my face toward the sea?*
>
> — Celtic prayer

Make arrangements with your bank to transfer funds internationally. Obtain traveler's checks and a hundred dollars' worth of foreign currency.

File a change of address with the post office and arrange for mail to be forwarded. Cancel magazine subscriptions that cannot be mailed overseas.

Discover as much as you can about your destination before you leave home. Try to learn at least a little of the language; sign up for a course or study on your own with tapes. Sample the foreign cuisine in a local restaurant.

Ask everyone you know for introductions to anyone from the country where you will be going. If you are moving because of a job, contact your company's human resources department to ask if they offer familiarization programs such as country briefings, cultural summaries, or foreign language classes.

Arrange an appointment with a relocation agency in the foreign country. Find out what items are hard to find or are more expensive abroad. Ask what items should be left at home.

Request absentee ballots for voting.

Contact the tourist board and the embassy of the country to which you are moving to request general information, free publications, travel tips, and street maps.

Dealing with Culture Shock

When you first arrive you're likely to be overwhelmed by sensations; at the very least, you'll be jet-lagged for the first few days. You'll be bombarded by the differences in food, water, language, customs, and social habits. "They" may drive on the "wrong" side of the road so even crossing a street can be dangerous. As you struggle to find your footing in a foreign land you'll experience culture shock, but you can minimize the discomfort by knowing what to expect.

Stage 1: Homesickness. Because everything is new and you are foreign, the loss of control heightens emotions. Faced with change and confusion on every level of daily life, most people are anxious, depressed, or moody for at least six months. Tempers will flare; any marital problems will be magnified. Adults may drink more heavily and children might revert to babyish behavior.

To deny that you're experiencing culture shock or act as if nothing's wrong will only delay your assimilation. Don't think that if only you (or your spouse or your kids) were better adjusted or more mature homesickness wouldn't happen. Everybody's homesick at first, even if they won't admit it.

Establish a routine as soon as possible; it'll help you feel grounded. Keep in touch with the folks at home; e-mail is a boon, especially if there's a major time difference. Don't expect family and friends to sympathize, though. Talk to local expatriates who will understand exactly how you feel because they've been through it.

Get all of the necessary activities out of the way as soon as possible. Register at the United States Consulate, the police, and local housing council. Open accounts with the bank and utility services. Apply for a local driver's license and parking permit. Check to see if you'll need a television license as well.

Recognize that everyone adjusts at his or her own pace. Be alert for signs that all is not well with your kids; difficulties with schoolwork or behavioral and health problems are all warnings. If things are really rough, don't hesitate to seek professional help. It's a myth that kids will adjust and problems will go away if you just ignore them.

Stage 2: Honeymoon. Now that you've got your bases covered — office and home set up, kids in school, pals who might become friends, and you know where to go for essentials and how to get there — it's time to spread your wings. Wearing your rose-colored glasses, you rush to explore and embrace the local culture. In this busy phase you try to see and do it all.

Stage 3: Readjustment. One day, after you've been in your new home for about a year, you suddenly feel settled. Life no longer feels like some bizarre extended vacation, and you stop trying to turn every experience into a meaningful memory. Suddenly, you're content to *be* as well as *do.* You accept that, although it's not like "home," this has become your home.

> *There are many places where I feel at home. Different homes echo with different parts of me: parts of me wake up in California, and parts of me wake up here in London. You can always feel like you're misplaced, or you can celebrate.*
>
> — Catherine Davidson

Coming Home

Robin Pascoe, in her book *Living and Working Abroad,* writes that re-entry can be harder than the initial move away. She warns that expatriates tend to idealize home and think that they can slide back into their old lives without any bumps. However, most people experience culture shock all over again when they return home.

Even if you're longing to go home it's unlikely to be the home that you left. Family members may have been born, graduated, gotten married, divorced, or died in your absence. Old friends may have made new friends. The neighborhood grocery store might have been demolished or a new golf course opened up. You might not know what people are talking about because of changes in society, politics, or fashion.

After such a life-changing experience, it'll be hard to understand that most folks don't really want to hear about your time abroad. If you only tell the good bits it sounds like you're bragging. If you talk about the difficulties it sounds like you're whining.

At such an unsettled stage, returning adults worry about the cost and chaos of setting up yet another household. Most are also anxious about finding or starting a new job. Not surprisingly, edgy emotions produce physical symptoms like headaches, stomachaches, insomnia, and nightmares in addition to jet lag. Take heart: Sooner or later (and it may take an entire year), you'll feel reconnected, and your life will be richer for the experience.

> *Being away is fine;*
> *being home is best.*
>
> — Swedish proverb

Index

1000 Country Household Hints
(Quigg), 83

Aloe for healing, 46

Balconies, 129–31
Balfour, Clara, 118
Baskets, 30, 34, 40, 43, 49
Bathrobes, 82
Bathrooms, 78–87, 124–25
Baxter, Richard, 7
Bedrooms, 65–74, 100–102,
  124–25
Beeton, Isabella, 11
Bells for housewarmings, 10–11
Benches, 59, 71
Binetti, Marianne, 127, 130
Birthdays away from home, 117
*Book of Household Management,
  The* (Beeton), 11
Boundary marking, 9
Bread gifts for abundance, 15
Breedlove, Greta, 80

Candles, 15, 30, 54, 58, 82
Capote, Truman, 113
Ceiling fans, 71
Centerpieces, 53
Children's rooms, 74–78
China, buying, 53
Christmas away from home,
  114–17
Circle of unity, 10
Closets, 69, 72, 73–74, 90
Coatracks, 31, 39, 87
Comforters, 67
Compass points for cleansing,
  16

Container gardening, 125–33
Culture shock, 149–51
Cunningham, Scott, 20, 67,
  80, 119
Curtains, 21, 69, 70, 86, 104,
  109

Davidson, Catherine, 151
Decorative accents, 59–61
Dining rooms, 49–54, 122–24
Door knockers, protective, 12
Doormats, personalizing, 35
Doors, 32–36
Dreams, 70–71

Eggs, symbol of hope, 14
Eiseman, Leatrice, 66
Entrances and exits, 24–40
Evergreens for doors, 33

Family trees, 37
Feather-shaped paper, wishes, 13
Feng shui, 4, 43, 47, 68, 87, 93,
  112, 135
Feng Shui Tips for a Better Life
  (Kennedy), 47
Fire for housewarmings, 6–8
Fireplaces, 42–44, 140
First footers, 10
Foreign country living, 146–52
Fountains, 14–15
Franklin, Benjamin, 88
Fuller, Sarah Margaret, 78
Furniture, 30, 38, 51, 57–58,
  74, 109, 110

Gardens, 125–36
Gates and doors, 32–36

Gay, John, 64
Gifts for housewarmings, 21–23
Goethe, Johann Wolfgang von, 98
Goldman, Emma, 122
Good-bye, saying, 138–39
Gould, Meredith, 95
Guest(s)
  books, 10, 40
  of housewarmings, 12–14
  rooms, 100–106
  rules for being a, 107–8

Hallways, 36–40, 121
Hand, symbol of protection, 13
Hanging baskets, 128, 130
Headboards, 66
Heart & Home (Pagram), 33
Herbal Home Spa, The (Breedlove), 80
Herbs, 46, 70, 121–22
Holidays, away for, 114–17
Home offices, 88–98, 124
Homes, 1–4. *See also* Houseplants; House-warmings; *specific rooms*
Homesickness, 149–50
Honeymoon, culture shock, 151
Horseshoes, protection, 14, 33
Host, being a gracious, 106–7
Hotel living, 112–14
House blessings, 14–16
Houseplants, 119–33
  container gardening, 125–33
  gardens, 133–36
  housewarming, 19–20, 21, 22
  indoor, 46, 47, 86, 96, 121–25
  temporary homes, 106, 110, 112, 115
Housewarmings, 5–23
  gifts for, 21–23
  holding, 6–16

sacred space, making, 17–21
symbols and meanings, 13

Jerome, Jerome K., 45
Journals of temporary homes, 111

Kennedy, David Daniel, 47, 112
Keys for guests, symbolic, 12
Kitchens, 44–49, 111, 121–22
Knight, Elizabeth, 12
Knock on Wood (Spencer), 46
Kristal, Jill, 138

L'Amour, Louis, 4
Lighting in homes, 37, 48, 62, 71, 74, 81, 92, 104
Living and Working Abroad (Pascoe), 151–52
Living rooms, 55–63
Long, Jim, 70
Longfellow, Henry Wadsworth, 41

Magical Household, The (Cunningham), 20, 67, 80, 119
Mailboxes, 26–27
Making a Living Without a Job (Winter), 89
Making Herbal Dream Pillows (Long), 70
Mattresses, 68, 104
Mirrors, 38, 43, 44, 56, 105
Monselet, Pierre-Charles, 55
Moore, Thomas, 16
Mortar and pestle, kitchen, 49
Moving into/out of homes, 137–52
Music, 53, 72, 83, 95, 104, 113
Musset, Alfred de, 96

Naming homes, 36
Napkins, 51
Nightstands, 71
Noise pollution, 95

Paget, Elizabeth, 103
Pagram, Beverly, 33
Painting, 36, 37, 50, 52,
    62–63, 84, 85, 93, 110
Pascoe, Robin, 151
Patios, 131–33
Pets and houseplants, 120
Phillpots, Eden, 137
Pictures and photos, 40, 60, 109
Pillows, 67, 70, 82, 104
Pineapple for hospitality, 35
Porches and portals, 27–31
Potpourri, 37, 38, 72, 115
Pounding for housewarmings,
    20

Quigg, Mary Roses, 83
Quilts, 67

Readjustment, culture shock,
    151
Rice and beans for prosperity, 8
Roethke, Theodore, 23
Rogue's gallery, 18
Rosemary for friendship, 34
Rugs, 38, 110

Sacred space, making, 17–21
Salt in homes, 15, 46
Seasonal changes, 61–62
Shadow-boxes, 60
Sheets, pink, 66
Shortcuts for Accenting Your
    Garden (Binetti), 127, 128
Showers, 83, 85
Slipcovers, 110
Smith, Sydney, 1
Soaps, 81

Spas, 81–83
Spencer, Linda, 46
Sprites, protection from, 14
Stairs, 39–40, 121
Stars and wishes, 20
Steps, entrance, 32
Stewart, Diana, 126
Swain, Charles, 5
Symbols, housewarmings, 13

Tables, 31, 47, 52, 58–59, 71
Tableware, 51
Tea drinking, 11–12, 98
Tea with Friends (Knight), 12
Telephones, 54, 83
Temporary homes, 99–117
Terraces, 129–31
Thanks, giving, 54
Thoreau, Henry David, 99
Time capsules, 15
"Touch-down surface," 38
Towels and racks, 80, 82, 84
Toys, 77
Trees for regeneration, 19
Twain, Mark, 24, 54
Two out of three rule, 50

Vanities, 72

Wharton, Edith, 135
Wicker for porches, 29
Wilde, Oscar, 69
Wind chimes, 31
Windowbox Book, The
    (Stewart), 126
Window boxes, 126–28
Windsocks, 36
Winter, Barbara, 89
Wordsworth, William, 21
Work environment, 88–98, 124
Working at Home (Gould), 95
Wreaths for doors, 34

Other Storey Books
You Will Enjoy

Feng Shui Tips for a Better Life, by David Daniel Kennedy. Learn how to use the ancient Chinese art of feng shui to attract desired life changes in the areas of health, romance, career opportunities, and more. 176 pages. Paperback. ISBN 1-58017-038-2.

Keeping Entertaining Simple, by Martha Storey. This fun-to-read tips book offers hundreds of ideas for low-fuss, low-anxiety entertaining with friends, for the holidays, and for business purposes. 176 pages. Paperback. ISBN 1-58017-056-0.

Keeping Fitness Simple, by Porter Shimer. A great guide to fun, easy fitness tips that don't involve expensive health clubs or exhausting workouts. 176 pages. Paperback. ISBN 1-58017-034-X.

Keeping Life Simple, by Karen Levine. This easy-to-read book helps readers assess what's really satisfying and then offers hundreds of tips for creating a lifestyle that is more rewarding. 160 pages. Paperback. ISBN 0-88266-943-5.

Keeping Work Simple, by Don Aslett and Carol Cartaino. Well-known time management expert and crusader against clutter, Don Aslett offers practical tips for simplifying any work environment to achieve maximum performance. 160 pages. Paperback. ISBN 0-88266-996-6.

Tea with Friends, by Elizabeth Knight. This beautifully illustrated book presents 12 months' worth of original, little-fuss party ideas to bring friends together around a pot of tea. Includes suggested menus, recipes, and decorations and activities for enhancing the celebration. 64 pages. Hardcover. ISBN 1-58017-050-1.

Unclutter Your Home, by Donna Smallin. This book offers hundreds of steps for sorting, evaluating, and getting rid of all those material items that get in the way of a simplified lifestyle. 192 pages. Paperback. ISBN 1-58017-108-7.

Working from Home, by Meredith Gould. Lively firsthand advice for creating the most comfortable, professional, and productive home office environment possible. 176 pages. Paperback. ISBN 1-58017-238-5.

These books and other Storey Books are available at your bookstore, farm store, garden center, or directly from Storey Books, Schoolhouse Road, Pownal, Vermont 05261, or by calling 1-800-441-5700. Or visit our Web site at www.storeybooks.com.